Spiritual Assassins

Defining and Driving out Unclean and Undesirable Spirits

By Pastor Bill Jenkins

Spiritual Assassins

Defining and Driving out Unclean and
Undesirable Spirits

By Pastor Bill Jenkins

All scripture quotations in this book are taken from the King James Version of the Bible unless otherwise noted.

Copyright © 2018
All Rights Reserved
978-0-692-08632-2

Published by:
Church of ACTS Publishing
3740 S. Dearborn St.
Indianapolis, IN 46237
www.churchofacts.org

Dedication

To my wife, Britain, I love you. Thank you for giving me uninterrupted time to study in order to do what I do.

TABLE OF CONTENTS

INTRODUCTION   1

CHAPTER 1   6
Six Levels of Satanic Influence

CHAPTER 2   16
Twenty Facts Concerning Spiritual Assassins

CHAPTER 3   21
Spiritual Assassins I
- Spirit of Bondage
- Deaf and Dumb Spirit
- Spirit of Haughtiness
- Spirit of Barrenness
- Spirit of Debt
- Spirit of Fear
- Spirit of Error
- Critical Spirit
- Spirit of Infirmity

CHAPTER 4   63
Spiritual Assassins II
- Spirit of Antichrist
- Spirit of Perversion
- A Lying Spirit
- Spirit of Slumber
- Spirit of Divination
- Spirit of Ishmael

Spirit of Korah
Seducing Spirits
Spirit of Jezebel

CHAPTER 5 — 102
Spiritual Assassins III

Spirit of Ahithophel
Spirit of Rebellion
Familiar Spirits
Spirit of Jealousy
Spirit of Heaviness
Spirit of Whoredom
Religious Spirit
Spirit of Absalom
Sprit of Saul

CHAPTER 6 — 135
Good Spirits of the Bible

CHAPTER 7 — 142
Keeping Your Freedom

CHAPTER 8 — 145
Spiritual Warfare Ammunition

CONCLUSION — 151

INTRODUCTION

Evil spirits are spiritual assassins who are trespassing on Holy Ground. A trespasser is one who unlawfully enters the territory of another. Trespassers can continue their unlawful practices until they are confronted and challenged on the basis of the law. The Bible is the law for the Christian. When we accept what Jesus did for us by dying on the Cross, the devil has no legal right to us. Hidden sin gives the devil legal right to stay. No demon can remain in our lives when we seriously desire him to go.

> *"Submit yourselves therefore to God. Resist the devil, and he will flee from you."* James 4:7

All Christians have been targeted for assassination by the enemy. There are spiritual assassins assigned to carry out the mission of the enemy to kill, steal, and destroy our lives. Even at birth the enemy assigns a demonic spirit, or an assassin, to us that if not detected and defeated, will cause us to wrestle with that spirit the rest of our lives. In Deuteronomy 28:45 we read, *"Moreover all these curses shall come upon thee, and shall pursue thee, and overtake thee, till thou be destroyed..."*

As targets of assassination by the enemy, we must realize that the devil will take significant events in our lives from our childhood, or past, and attempt to control our minds, and our lives, to keep us in bondage. The devil assigns assassins to our:

- Finances
- Marriage
- Children
- Cars
- Jobs
- Friends
- Memories
- Homes
- Minds

Anyone who is saved, and has a heart to be more like Jesus, is a target. Some Biblical examples of targets of assassination are:

- Saul - The Spirit of the Lord departed from Saul, and an evil spirit troubled Saul in 1 Samuel 16:14.

- Paul - Paul said there was a thorn in the flesh; *"...the messenger of Satan sent to buffet me,"* in 2 Corinthians 12:7.

- Jesus - Even Jesus was a target of assassination by the devil in the wilderness in Luke 4.

This book is designed to be a tool to help in defining, describing, and driving out unclean and undesirable trespassers. The ultimate purpose of all evil spirits is to separate you from fulfilling your destiny. You must get militant about obtaining your freedom.

It is very important to be conscious of your spiritual condition on a daily basis. One of my favorite scriptures is 1 Corinthians 11:31, *"For if we would judge ourselves, we should not be judged."* Judge yourself to determine your need for deliverance.

Two Ways to Know if You Need Deliverance:
1. **Discernment** – to know by the Spirit
2. **Detection** – to know by the symptoms

Only God can give discernment, but this book can help you detect the symptoms, so you can be aware never to allow Satan to gain an advantage.

A pastor was getting really fed up with his wife's over-spending. He decided he was going to do something about it. He knew she needed a new dress, so he told her she could only spend $100. He reminded her that if she was tempted to spend more, just say, "Satan, get thee behind me!" His wife left to go shopping and finally returned home after several hours. She had a beautiful new dress to show to her husband. He said, "Wow that is quite a dress for $100!" She replied, "Oh, it was only $250!" Frustrated, he said, "You spent $250 on a dress?!!" Didn't you say, 'Satan, get thee behind me like I told you?" She said, "Well, yes, I did say that, and Satan told me it looked good from back there too!"

This story is an example of how we accommodate the devil instead of confronting him. Even when Jesus was tempted by the devil, He did not accommodate him, but confronted him with the Word of God. The Word of God is not only your legal way to keep demons from entering your life, but it's also your hedge to keep them out of your life.

> *"...and whoso breaketh an hedge, a serpent shall bite him."* Ecclesiastes 10:8

In the Old Testament, there was a special kind of hedge that was planted around the house to keep dangerous, poisonous, and deadly snakes from coming onto the property and houses. The smallest break or opening in the hedge would allow the snake in to harm the people. The Word of God is your hedge to keep out the snakes.

You must stay connected to the Lord, walk in obedience to God's word, and close any gaps that could be created by your disobedience and sin. As long as you are aware of the devil's devices, and stay in full pursuit of God's righteousness in your life, you will never have to be devil-conscious in your life. Be God-conscious, and know God has destined you for complete victory.

> *"He that committeth sin is of the devil; for*

the devil sinneth from the beginning. For this purpose the Son of God was manifested, that he might destroy the works of the devil." 1 John 3:8

CHAPTER 1

SIX LEVELS OF SATANIC INFLUENCE

There are different levels, or degrees, of demonic bondage. To whatever degree we are ignorant of the devil's devices, is to the degree we will be in bondage to the enemy. The enemy is sly in gaining access into our lives in order to gain an advantage.

3 Ways Satan Gains Access:
1. **Sin**
2. **Life Circumstances**
3. **Inheritance**

Once the devil gains access, he wants to have as much control of your heart as possible. The devil wants full control by possessing your life totally, and a lot of damage can be done by the enemy along the way. It is incumbent upon you to use godly discernment to recognize the efforts of the devil to stop his advancement in your life sooner rather than later. There are six levels of a progressive satanic bondage that attempt to negatively affect your life.

Six Levels of Bondage

1. Regression

Regression is not just going backwards but an act of reasoning backwards. In other words, you come to the conclusion that it's ok to retreat. You begin to make sense of returning to your sinful ways. Satan is good at sending people to hurt you, offend you, and lie about you. He is also good at getting you to over-think, or under-think, things that will get you to stop moving forward and keep you from serving God. Satan wants you to *regress,* but God's plan is for you to *progress*. If Satan can get you even to take one step backwards, you are on your way to being under his control. It's subtle and slow, but make no mistake about it, it's where the enemy starts to gain an advantage.

In order to avoid regressing in your relationship with God, you must pursue the Lord, and be renewed in your Spirit on a daily basis. Paul said in 2 Corinthians 4:16, *"...our outward man perish, yet the inward man is renewed day by day."* In other words, your mind and spirit are not

> *Satan wants you to regress; God's plan is for you to progress.*

supposed to wrinkle like your body. You cannot allow the enemy to convince you that the older you get, the worse you get or that the older you get, the less you do. Proverbs 4:18 states, *"But the path of the just is as the shining light, that shineth more and more unto the perfect day."* God expects progress and production. Don't allow the enemy to convince you to slow down, back off, or stop your pursuit of God. You should always chase after God to close the gap, and minimize the distance, between you and the Lord. One of the greatest lessons I learned when I began my ministry was, whatever you feed will grow, and whatever you starve will die. Feed your Spirit on the things of God, and you won't go backwards. God is not a God of regression or retreat; He is a God of progression and advancement.

2. **Suppression**

Suppression means to put down by force. It's when something happens that is bad in your life, and instead of dealing with it in prayer, you ignore it and attempt to deny its existence.

The enemy is trying to keep you ignorant. He wants to minimize the effect of what life can sometimes bring to you. He doesn't want you to know you can be free and whole. He wants you to accept the unacceptable. He wants you to accept the abnormal as normal. The devil desires for you to try to deny the existence of personal issues that need to be dealt with, so you will not truly experience freedom in the Lord.

People in a state of suppression often can be:
- **Unteachable**: They do not listen to good advice. *"Whoso loveth instruction loveth knowledge: but he that hateth reproof is a brutish."* Proverbs 12:1
- **Weak in Mind**: *"A wise man is strong; yea, a man of knowledge increaseth strength."* Proverbs 24:5
- **Selfish:** When you are only thinking of yourself. *"Teach me good judgment and knowledge: for I have believed thy commandments."* Psalm 119:66
- **Ignorant**: When you don't know better, you can't be better. *"My people are destroyed for lack of knowledge..."* Hosea 4:6

You are only as sick as your secrets, so don't ignore or deny the obvious. Take your burdens to the Lord, and be healed.

3. **Oppression**
Oppression means to weigh someone down with something that cannot be carried. It's prolonged, cruel, and unjust treatment. You are not built to carry your own load. 1 Peter 5:7 states, *"casting all your cares [all your anxieties, all your worries, and all your concerns, once and for all] on Him, for He cares about you [with deepest affection, and*

watches over you very carefully]." (Amplified version) The temptations and trials you face are no different than anyone else's. But the devil is good at lying to you and telling you that no one is going through things like you. Oppression makes you feel overwhelmed. It takes your breath away and causes your mind to wander to places of hopelessness. God is faithful and will not allow you to be tempted beyond what you can bear.

4. **Obsession**

   Obsession is a compulsive preoccupation with a fixed idea or unwanted feeling, thought, or emotion that is accompanied by anxiety. It's something that has a hold of you that you can't shake. It's something that consumes your time and controls your life. It makes you suspicious and paranoid. It's the topic of every conversation you have. It rules you from the moment you wake until the moment you fall asleep. It can bring nightmares and cause you not to feel rested.

5. **Depression**

   Depression is a mental state of altered mood, characterized by feelings of sadness, despair, and discouragement. It's not just a medical condition, but a spiritual condition, that must be addressed with prayer, professional help, and counseling. You can't "will" your way out of true depression. You need to truly overcome the enemy.

6. **Possession**

Demon possession is the full control of an individual by demons that change the personality, alters the voice, and/or inflicts personal injury. It is the owning of a personality. Demon possession means that a new personality is introduced to that person. The victim becomes a different person. The demon of Gadarene acted and spoke as one who was controlled by another personality: Matthew 8:29, *"And, behold, they cried out, saying, What have we to do with thee, Jesus, thou Son of God? art thou come hither to torment us before the time?"* They possess supernatural knowledge. Now, most people do not get to a place of demonic possession, but it is the goal of the devil.

Characteristics of Demon Possession
Mark 5:1-20

- Indwelling of an Unclean Spirit, v. 2
  Unclean spirits enter where there is continual unrepentant sin.
- Infatuated with Death and Darkness, v.3
- Unusual Physical Strength, v. 3-4
- Reckless and Undisciplined Personality, v. 4
- Constantly Inflicting Pain on Yourself, v. 5
- Splitting of the Personality, v. 6-7
  One minute he was afraid, and the next minute he was worshipping Jesus.

- A Resistance to Spiritual Things, v. 7
- Alteration of Voice, v. 9

One truth Christians need to embrace is the need to quit accepting unreasonable situations, and reoccurring problems, as just a normal part of life. Trouble will happen in your life, but to be continually harassed and irritated by different issues might be nothing more than the devil keeping you from experiencing abundant life in Christ. Below is a list of different manifestations that you need to stop tolerating and get delivered from in your life.

Other Demonic Manifestations

- **Emotional Problems**
  Emotional disturbances which persist or recur such as resentment, hatred, anger, fear, rejection, feeling unwanted or unloved, self-pity, jealousy, depression, stress, inferiority, and insecurity

- **Mental Problems**
  Disturbances in mind or thought life such as mental torment, indecision, procrastination, nervous breakdowns, worry, compromise, confusion, doubt, loss of memory, thinking too much, and rationalization

- **Speech Problems**
  Outburst, uncontrolled use of tongue, lying, sarcasm, cursing, negative speech, blasphemy, mockery, criticism, gossip, and murmuring

- **Financial Problems**
  Misuse of money, cheating, gambling, not tithing, poverty, embezzlement, debt, bankruptcy, job layoffs, cars not working properly, and things breaking down or not lasting long enough

- **Sex Problems**
  Recurring unclean thoughts and actions, fantasies, lust, incest, masturbation, homosexuality, fornication, adultery, pornography, provocativeness, and lack of desire

- **Addictions**
  Nicotine, alcohol, drugs, medicines, caffeine, sugar, food, TV, video games, and even people

- **Physical Infirmities**
  Many diseases and sicknesses are due to spirits of infirmity: heartburn, colds, headaches, allergies, arthritis, and back pain

- **Religious Error**
  Involvement in religious error opens the door for demons. False religions, "Christian" cults (Jehovah Witnesses, Mormons, Christian Scientist), and groups that deny the necessity of the blood of Christ for salvation; ESP or extrasensory perception, or Ouija boards, levitation, astrology, witchcraft, séances, and tarot cards

- **Accident Prone**
  Cutting yourself, hitting your head, falling downstairs, choking on food, burning yourself, car accidents, being bitten by dogs, and bumping into doors (One accident doesn't mean you're cursed, but if it is several or consistently, praying doesn't hurt.)

- **Female Problems**
  Barrenness, miscarriages, tumors, pain during intercourse, growths, lack of desire, excessive bleeding, and lumps in breasts

- **Martial Problems**
  Constant arguing, fighting, separation, divorce, disagreements, and strife

There are many ways the enemy will attempt to bring down the child of God. You must be alert to identifying the attack of the enemy as quickly as possible. After identifying the problem, you will have a clearer idea as to how to approach the situation to achieve victory in your life.

> *Whatever you feed will grow; whatever you starve will die.*

"No, in all these things we are more than conquerors through him who loved us."
Romans 8:37 NIV

CHAPTER

*TWENTY FACTS CONCERNING
SPIRITUAL ASSASSINS*

---

1. **They have Names**

   "And Jesus asked him, saying, What is thy name? And he said, Legion: because many devils were entered into him." Luke 8:30

2. **They Speak**

   "When he saw Jesus, he cried out, and fell down before him, and with a loud voice said, What have I to do with thee, Jesus, thou Son of God most high? I beseech thee, torment me not." Luke 8:28

3. **They Know Who Jesus is**

   "Saying, Let us alone; what have we to do with thee, thou Jesus of Nazareth? art thou come to destroy us? I know thee who thou art; the Holy One of God." Luke 4:34

4. **They Know Who You are**

   "And the evil spirit answered and said, Jesus I know, and Paul I know; but who are ye?" Acts 19:15

5. **They Possess Great Strength**

   "Who had his dwelling among the tombs; and no man could bind him, no, not with chains: Because that he had been often bound with fetters and chains, and the chains had been plucked asunder by him, and the fetters broken in pieces: neither could any man tame him." Mark 5:3-4

6. **They Experience Fear**

   "When he saw Jesus, he cried out, and fell down before him, and with a loud voice said, What have I to do with thee, Jesus, thou Son of God most high? I beseech thee, torment me not." Luke 8:28

7. **They Have Evil Personalities**

   "And wheresoever he taketh him, he teareth him: and he foameth, and gnasheth with his teeth, and pineth away: and I spake to thy disciples that they should cast him out; and they could not." Mark 9:18

8. They Enter Through Open Doors

"And when he was come out of the ship, immediately there met him out of the tombs a man with an unclean spirit," Mark 5:2

9. They Can Influence Our Speech

"And when the devil was cast out, the dumb spake: and the multitudes marvelled, saying, It was never so seen in Israel." Matthew 9:33

10. They are Not All-Powerful or All-Knowing

"But of that day and hour knoweth no man, no, not the angels of heaven, but my Father only." Matthew 24:36

11. They Cause Suicidal Tendencies

"And ofttimes it hath cast him into the fire, and into the waters, to destroy him: but if thou canst do any thing, have compassion on us, and help us." Mark 9:22

12. They Oppose God's Purpose

"For we wrestle not against flesh and blood, but against principalities, against powers, against the rulers of the darkness of this

world, against spiritual wickedness in high places." Ephesians 6:12

13. They Carry Out Satan's Program

"Now the Spirit speaketh expressly, that in the latter times some shall depart from the faith, giving heed to seducing spirits, and doctrines of devils;" 1 Timothy 4:1

14. They Cause Deafness

"When Jesus saw that the people came running together, he rebuked the foul spirit, saying unto him, Thou dumb and deaf spirit, I charge thee, come out of him, and enter no more into him." Mark 9:25

15. They Spread False Doctrine

"That ye be not soon shaken in mind, or be troubled, neither by spirit, nor by word, nor by letter as from us, as that the day of Christ is at hand." 2 Thessalonians 2:2

16. They Cause Disease (lack of ease)

"And when he had called unto him his twelve disciples, he gave them power against unclean spirits, to cast them out, and to heal all manner of sickness and all

manner of disease." Matthew 10:1

17. They Cause Personal Injury

"And wheresoever he taketh him, he teareth him: and he foameth, and gnasheth with his teeth, and pineth away: and I spake to thy disciples that they should cast him out; and they could not." Mark 9:18

18. They Cause Blindness

"Then was brought unto him one possessed with a devil, blind, and dumb: and he healed him, insomuch that the blind and dumb both spake and saw." Matthew 12:22

19. They Will be Judged

"Know ye not that we shall judge angels? how much more things that pertain to this life?" 1 Corinthians 6:3

20. They Will Eventually be Cast in the Lake of Fire with the Devil

"Then shall he say also unto them on the left hand, Depart from me, ye cursed, into everlasting fire, prepared for the devil and his angels:" Matthew 25:41

CHAPTER

SPIRITUAL ASSASSINS I

SPIRIT OF BONDAGE
Romans 8:15-16

"For ye have not received the spirit of bondage again to fear, but ye have received the Spirit of adoption, whereby we cry, Abba Father. The spirit itself beareth witness with our spirit, that we are the children of God:"

The Spirit of Bondage is anything that binds you to the point where you become an involuntary slave. It causes you to feel like you have lost your ability to make a reasonable godly choice. In Romans 8:15-16, there are three spirits mentioned:

1. **Spirit of Bondage**
2. **Spirit of Adoption**
3. **Human Spirit**

The human spirit is the deciding factor as to which of these two spirits dominates your life. There are two forces at work: the driving of the flesh and the leading of

> *The human spirit is the deciding factor.*

the Spirit. They are at war for your soul. You choose to be in bondage to the devil and your flesh, or you can accept the fact that Jesus wants to adopt you. When you are adopted, you lose all rights and privileges of the old family and gain all the rights and privileges of the new family.

"Therefore if any man be in Christ, he is a new creature: old things are passed away; behold, all things are become new." 2 Corinthians 5:17

If Christ is in your heart, you need to let Him possess your life and not be controlled by anything that makes you an involuntary slave. Addiction is a powerful force and the only way to overcome it is with the help of God.

Characteristics of the Spirit of Bondage

- Drug abuse
- Alcoholism
- Smoking
- Food addictions
- Sexual immorality
- Watching too much television
- Swearing and cussing
- Past Experiences
- Pornography
- Eating disorders
- Video games
- Listening to bad music

- Caffeine addiction
- Abusive behavior
- Fear
- Religion
- Selfish ambition
- Depression
- Family curses
- Debt

You can be in bondage to just about anything. One way to determine the depth of bondage is evaluating the amount of time, money, and attention that you are spending participating in certain activities. Hiding, denying, dismissing, underestimating, and excusing are all signs that only provide proof of bondage. If you find you are spending a large amount of time on something, and denying its negative influence, or claiming you could quit when you want to, it might be you're in bondage.

Three C's Of Addiction
Romans 7:15-19

1. **Compulsion,** v. 15
   Compulsion is an irresistible, repeated, and irrational impulse to perform some act. *"For that which I do I allow not: for what I would, that do I not; but what I hate, that do I."*

2. **Control Loss,** v. 18
   Control loss is the lack of ability to exercise authority over something. *"For I know that in me (that is, in my flesh,) dwelleth no good thing: for to will is present with me; but how to perform that which is good I find not."*

3. Continued Use, v. 19
"For the good that I would I do not: but the evil which I would not, that I do."

If there is compulsive behavior that makes you feel you have lost control of making godly decisions, and you can't stop something you want to stop, then you are in bondage to it and need deliverance immediately.

How to Assassinate the Assassin of Bondage
Matthew 16:13-19

Get a firsthand revelation of who Christ is in verses 13-17. He is the Anointed One who destroys every yoke and removes all burdens. This revelation brought a demonstration of God that lead to the annihilation of the devil. God has given you keys to unlock, bind, or loose, in verse 19.

Learn to Use Your Keys:

- **Prayer**
- **Praise and Worship**
- **Word of God**
- **Name of Jesus**
- **Words of Your Mouth**

Bind: Spirit of Bondage
Loose: Spirit of Recognition and Liberty
Read: Galatians 5:1; John 8:32

DUMB AND DEAF SPIRIT
Mark 9:17-29

"And one of the multitude answered and said, Master, I have brought unto thee my son, which hath a dumb spirit;"

Dumb and Deaf Spirit is the name of one spirit, but it causes many problems. It's not the people that make themselves do things that are not smart but the Dumb and Deaf Spirit. This spirit attempts to attach itself mostly to children and youth. The demon seizes them, takes them by force, and compels them to do certain things and go to certain places, in order to destroy their lives to the point where they are unproductive in society; or, it attempts to kill them outright. The enemy wants them to do something foolish at an early age that can impact the rest of their lives. A Dumb and Deaf Spirit is almost always involved in:

- Teen pregnancy
- Suicides
- Peer pressure to drink, smoke, or do drugs
- Molestation of children
- Teen runaways
- Teenage prostitution
- Teen robbery and violence
- Rebellion
- Listening to bad music groups
- Teen car accidents

- Accidental killings and murders
- Gang Involvement
- Lack of comprehension
- Keeping people from coming to Christ
- Learning disorders and ADD
- Accident prone
- Silly pranks
- Risky behavior

Parents, you must pray for, and over, your children daily. You need to understand the devil wants your kids more than he wants you sometimes. You have to cooperate with God to keep your children safe in every way.

The #1 spirit attacking our youth is a Dumb & Deaf Spirit.

Characteristics of a Dumb and Deaf Spirit

- Physical blindness, Matthew 12:22; or eye diseases not caused by aging
- Spiritual blindness
- Burns, Mark 9:22
- Gnashing teeth, Mark 9:18
- Mental illness, Matthew 17:15; Mark 5:5
- Seizures and epilepsy, Mark 9:18, 20, & 26
- Constant crying, Mark 9:26

- Ear problems, Mark 9:25
- Muteness, Luke 11:14; Mark 9:25
- Drowning, Mark 9:22
- Lots of accidents, Mark 9
- Suicidal tendencies, Mark 9:22
- Bruising, Luke 9:39
- Lack of comprehension
- Being disruptive during church services, weddings, and movies, in homes, families, and with other children (i.e. fiddling with things, going to the bathroom, and a tendency to talk at inappropriate times)
- Compulsive personality
- Low attention span

How to Assassinate the Assassin of A Dumb and Deaf Spirit

The story from Mark 9:17-29 demonstrates that children are bothered by, and can even be controlled or possessed by, demons. Jesus told this father he must cooperate with Him, in two areas, in order for his boy to be delivered:

1. **Naturally**
   Don't tell your kids one thing and then do another. Don't tell them to stop doing drugs with a beer and cigarette in your hand. Deal with rebellion and stubbornness while they are still babies instead of waiting till they are

teenagers. Enforce consequences on negative behavior, but do it correctly.

2. **Spiritually**

   Spiritually, the father needed to pray and fast for his child's continued deliverance. Prayer demonstrates your reliance on God even in impossible situations. Your kids' survival in this world depends on you making the time to pray, and take dominion over evil forces before they get snatched away from you. Put them in a spiritual environment by bringing them to church and creating a Christian environment in your home.

All good parents want a better life for their children than they had themselves. It's imperative that you monitor your kids' behavior and control their influences to ensure their well-being. It's also important to look to the Word of God for guidance in raising them, and cooperate with the Lord in fulfilling your obligation as parents.

> *"Train up a child in the way he should go: and when he is old, he will not depart from it."* Proverbs 22:6

Bind: Dumb and Deaf Spirit
Loose: Resurrection Life and Gifts of Healing
Read: Romans 8:11; 1 Corinthians 12:9

SPIRIT OF HAUGHTINESS
Proverbs 16:18-19

"Pride goeth before destruction and an haughty spirit before a fall. Better it is to be of an humble spirit with the lowly, than to divide the spoil with the proud."

Haughtiness is pride. It is blatantly and disdainfully displaying an attitude towards others because you believe you are better, smarter, or more important than someone else. It is an attitude of superiority. Make no mistake about it; the devil is not a negative "god" but a fallen angel who fell because of pride. Just as it did with the devil, this prideful spirit attempts to rob you of God's best for your life.

"How art thou fallen from heaven, O Lucifer, son of the morning! How art thou cut down to the ground, which didst weaken the nations! For thou hast said in thine heart, I will ascend into heaven, I will exalt my throne above the stars of God: I will sit also upon the mount of the congregation, in the sides of the north: I will ascend above the heights of the clouds; I will be like the most High. Yet thou shalt be brought down to hell, to the sides of the pit. They that see thee shall narrowly look upon thee, and consider thee, saying, Is this the man that made the

earth to tremble, that did shake kingdoms;"
Isaiah 14:12-16

Pride makes you falsely believe you are better than others and creates a sense of entitlement that others somehow owe you something. Pride is often recognized by others before you recognize it yourself. Pride is destructive, deceitful, and deadly.

Four Kinds of Pride

1. **Class Pride** - Think they are better because of their house, clothes, neighborhood or job.

2. **Racial Pride** - Think they are superior because of the color of their skin.

3. **Intellectual Pride** - Think they are better because of their education.

4. **Religious Pride** - Think they are better because of their spiritual experience.

Examples of the Spirit of Haughtiness

- Pharaoh
  Exodus 5:2, *"And Pharaoh said, Who is the Lord, that I should obey his voice to let Israel go? I know not the Lord; neither will I let Israel go."*

- Naaman
    2 Kings 5:9-11; Naaman wanted Elisha, and not his servant, to pray for him. He was upset about how and where the miracle had to come from.

- Nebuchadnezzar
    Daniel 3:10-30; Nebuchadnezzar turned the fire up seven times hotter because the three Hebrew children would not bow down to him. They came out of the fire and had not been touched. Jesus went into the fire with them.

Characteristics of a Spirit of Haughtiness

- Arrogance, 2 Samuel 22:28
- Boastful, 1 Peter 5:5
- Strife, Proverbs 28:25
- Unteachable
- Self-Righteous, Luke 18:11,12
- Anger, Proverbs 21:24
- Contentious, Proverbs 13:10
- Vanity
- Egotistic
- Gossiping
- Stubborn, Proverbs 29:1
- Overbearing, domineering, and controlling

Pride is one of the three major sins that you will face and have to battle to overcome your entire life. It is difficult, but not impossible, to get the victory over pride. It's going to take hard work to notice it when it arises. When you do, quickly humble yourself, so it's not allowed to take a greater hold on you. When you notice it rising, begin to act on these four principles to help remain humble in your life.

How to Assassinate the Assassin of Haughtiness

1. **Foot Washing,** John 13:4-16
   Jesus set an example that washing feet is a way to bring humility.

2. **Serving Others,** Mark 10:44
   Humble yourself by serving.

3. **Fasting,** Psalm 35:13
   The psalmist said, *"I humbled my soul with fasting."*

4. **Accountability,** Ephesians 5:21
   "Submitting yourselves one to another." Ask someone to tell you when you act in pride or are being prideful.

Bind: Spirit of Pride
Loose: Spirit of Humility
Read: James 4:10; Proverbs 22:4; 1 Peter 5:6

SPIRIT OF BARRENNESS
Exodus 23:25-26

"And ye shall serve the Lord your God, and he shall bless thy bread and thy water; and I will take sickness away from the midst of thee. There shall nothing cast their young, nor be barren, in thy land: the number of thy days I will fulfil."

Barrenness means to hold back, to lock up, to shut out, and to be unproductive. In the Old Testament a childless woman was considered a failure. Her barrenness was a social embarrassment to her husband. The Bible records seven women who were barren. Six of the seven had their barrenness turned around. David's wife, Michal, was the only woman who never had her barrenness turned. She despised what God valued, and the Lord did not want that spirit to be reproduced in a child. Let's take a closer look at each case of barrenness.

Sarah
Sarah is Abraham's wife. We read of her barrenness in Genesis 11:30 and in Romans 4:19. Sarah's womb was noted as being "dead". However, in Genesis 21:1-2, we read of her barrenness being turned. In Romans 4:20, Abraham staggered not at the promise of God through unbelief, but was strong in faith, giving glory to God, and being fully persuaded that what He had promised, He was able to perform. You see, Sarah's faith in God turned her barrenness as we note in Hebrews 11:6, *"But without*

faith it is impossible to please Him."

Rebekkah
Isaac's wife was barren for 20 years, but as it reads in Genesis 25:21, *"Isaac intreated the Lord for his wife."* Rebekkah was prophesied to be the mother of thousands of millions, and her seed would possess the gate of her enemy. Intercessory prayer turned her barrenness.

Rachel
Jacob's wife, Rachel, was barren. Genesis 30:1 tells of her barrenness. Rachel envied her sister and was desperate. In verse one she said, *"Give me children or else I die."* In verse 22 it states, *"And God remembered Rachel, and God hearkened to her, and opened her womb."* Her desperation turned her barrenness.

Manoah's Wife
When Samson's mother, or Manoah's wife, was found to be barren, she was visited by an angel of the Lord in Judges 13:3-4. *"Behold now, thou art barren, and bearest not: but thou shalt conceive, and bear a son. Now therefore beware, I pray thee, and drink not wine nor strong drink, and eat not any unclean thing:"* She was given instructions, and she followed them. Her obedience turned her barrenness.

Hannah

In 1 Samuel 1:5, it tells of Hannah's barrenness. She consistently prayed, *"Give me a child, and I'll give him back,"* 1 Samuel 1:11. She went to Eli sobbing so badly he thought she was drunk for, *"The Spirit maketh intercession with groanings which cannot be uttered,"* Romans 8:26. Just as we see in Romans 4:17, *"Call those things that be not as though they were."* A prophetic word turned her barrenness.

Elizabeth

We are told us of Elizabeth's barrenness in Luke 1:7. She did everything right but still was barren. Even when everything seems lined up, it must be God's timing. *"He hath made every thing beautiful in his time:"* Ecclesiastes 3:11. The custom was to name a child after his father, but God said to call him John. Do not put your name on what God does. *"For my thoughts are not your thoughts, neither are your ways my ways, saith the Lord."* Isaiah 55:8. The timing of God turned her barrenness.

Michal

There was only one woman in the Bible who didn't have her barrenness turned around. Michal, David's wife, despised what God valued, and God decided to allow her to remain barren because He did not want that spirit reproduced.

Is your spirit worth reproducing?

It's not God's will for you to be locked up and held back from fulfilling your destiny. It is not God's will for His people to be barren. Allow the Spirit of Barrenness to be broken off over your life as you yield to the Holy Spirit.

Characteristics of Barrenness

- Unproductive
- Unfruitful
- Close mindedness
- Weariness
- Lack of desire
- Fear
- Disobedience
- Indifferent
- Careless

How to Assassinate the Assassin of Barrenness

1. **Sarah** = Faith in God
2. **Rebekkah** = Intercessory Prayer
3. **Rachel** = Desperation
4. **Manoah's Wife** = Obedience
5. **Hannah** = Prophetic Word
6. **Elizabeth** = God's Timing

Bind: Spirit of Barrenness
Loose: Love, Power, and Sound Mind
Read: 2 Peter 5:7-10

SPIRIT OF DEBT
Haggai 1:5-6, 1 Samuel 22:1-2

"Now therefore thus saith the Lord of hosts; Consider your ways. Ye have sown much, and bring in little; ye eat, but ye have not enough; ye drink, but ye are not filled with drink; ye clothe you, but there is none warm; and he that earneth wages earneth wages to put it into a bag with holes."

How and what you spend your money on is a clear indication of where your priorities lie. Jesus had strong opinions about money; in fact, He talked more about money than He talked about Heaven or Hell. One of the ways you demonstrate your commitment to Christ is through the distribution of your financial resources.

Seven Signs of Financial Bondage

1. **When Married Couples Argue Over Finances**
   Proverbs 15:27, *"He that is greedy for gain troubleth his own house."* Satan wants to distract couples from serving the Lord by focusing on money problems. Constant arguing over basic bills, how much is coming in, how money is being spent, and getting mad over spouses purchases of items are a sure sign of financial bondage. The number one cause of divorce is money trouble.

2. **Putting Daily Expenditures on Charge Cards due to a Lack of Funds**
   1 John 2:15 *"Love not the world, neither the things that are in the world."* Driving a nice car, living in a big home, wearing nice clothes is *not* a sign of God's blessing on your life. If you put food, gas, or clothes on a credit card, and cannot pay it off in full the next month, you are in bondage.

3. **Putting off a Bill from One Month to Another**
   Proverbs 22:1, *"A good name is to be chosen than great riches."* Putting off paying our bills hurts your witness and gives God a black eye. 82% of Americans claim to be Christian, yet bankruptcy, debt, and foreclosures are at an all-time high.

4. **Borrowing to Pay Fixed Expenses**
   Proverbs 19:1, *"Better is the poor that walketh in his integrity, than he that is perverse in his lips, and is a fool."* Living above your means is wrong and foolish, and no amount of refinancing will help. Borrowing to pay for fixed expenses is a sure sign you don't have a budget.

5. **Becoming Unaware of How Much You Owe**
   Proverbs 27:23, *"Be thou diligent to know the state of thy flocks."* Most people don't have a budget and have no idea what they owe and where all their money goes. People just say, "I

don't want to know how bad it is."

6. **When You Begin to Entertain Thoughts of Dishonesty in Finances**
   1 Timothy 6:10, *"For the Love of money is the root of all evil."* Money isn't bad; the *love* of it is because it can cause a person to travel to "gray" areas of life.

7. **When You Find it Difficult to Tithe**
   Malachi 3:8, *"Will a man rob God?"* In Matthew 23:23, Jesus commends the Pharisees for tithing and says you should do it.

Characteristics of Financial Bondage

- Excessive debt
- Overdue bills
- Overspending
- Greed
- Coveting
- Resentment when others are blessed
- Get rich quick attitude
- Anger when offerings are taken
- Not planning for future
- Consumed with thinking about money
- Cannot sleep
- Constant borrowing of money
- Lack of regular giving

- Irresponsible
- Discontent
- Worry
- Unsatisfied
- Deceitful
- Laziness
- No stability on job
- Delinquent accounts
- Mishandling of funds
- Impulsive behavior
- Can't make minimum payments
- Maxed out credit cards
- No vision of financial future

How to Assassinate the Assassin of Debt

There are three types of giving that will produce freedom:

1. **Systematic Giving**
   God asks us to contribute a certain percentage of our income on a regular basis. *"Upon the first day of the week let every one of you lay by him in store,"* 1 Corinthians 16:2a

   Malachi 3:10 tells us four things about tithing:
   1) The What: Your whole tithe which is 10% of your income. This means before the government takes theirs (i.e. gross income).

2) **The Where:** You are to give to the storehouse. What is your storehouse? It is where you get spiritual food - your home church.

3) **The Why:** The Lord says to test Him. Testing will prove or determine the value. Do a 90 day trial. Mark down and journal the blessings over those 90 days - things that happen for your good and things that don't happen.

4) **The Wow:** Tithing will bring blessing. Blessing you won't have room enough to contain. *"Now to Him who is able to do immeasurably more than all we ask or imagine..."* Ephesians 3:20 (NIV)

Jesus talked more about giving than He did about Heaven or Hell.

---

2. Spontaneous Giving
There are times on an impromptu basis when we are encouraged to offer our own resources to meet a specific need.

> *"What good is it, my brothers and sisters, if someone claims to have faith but has no deeds? Can such faith save them? Suppose a brother or a sister is without clothes and daily food. If one of you says to them, "Go in peace; keep warm and well fed," but does nothing about their physical needs, what good is it? In the same way, faith by itself, if it is not accompanied by action, is dead."* James 2:14-17 (NIV)

> *"He that hath pity upon the poor lendeth unto the Lord; and that which he hath given will he pay him again."* Proverbs 19:17

We also see in Matthew 25:31-46, that giving is one way God uses to determine the sheep from the goats.

3. Sacrificial Giving

Sacrificial giving is offering above and beyond what you think you can afford. Sacrificial giving is seed giving. But keep in mind, God never asks anything of you He hasn't already done. He sent His one and only Son to take your place. He sent Jesus, whose Father is the King of Kings; He didn't live in poverty before coming.

> *"For ye know the grace of our Lord Jesus*

Christ, that, though he was rich, yet for your sakes he became poor, that ye through his poverty might be rich." 2 Corinthians 8:9

Learning to give of your finances through tithes and offerings is a great way to begin to get out of debt. You must also be disciplined in your spending habits. Never spend more than what you make.

Bind: Spirit of Debt
Loose: Spirit of Prosperity and Wisdom
Read: Proverbs 14:24; Ezekiel 28:4-5

SPIRIT OF FEAR
2 Timothy 1:7

"For God hath not given us a spirit of fear; but of power, and of love, and of a sound mind."

Two Kinds of Fear

1. **Positive Fear**
   To have a positive fear of something is to have a deep respect for it. You should respect and obey the laws of electricity and fire. If you don't, you will get hurt. It is the same way with a fear of God. If you respect Him by obeying His laws, you won't get hurt eternally. What does it mean to fear or respect the Lord?

   - **Hate Evil**
     Proverbs 8:13, *"The fear of the Lord is to hate evil."*
   - **Walk in Wisdom**
     Psalm 111:10, *"The fear of the Lord is the beginning of wisdom..."*
   - **Be Blessed**
     Psalm 115:13, *"He will bless them that fear the Lord,"*
   - **Salvation**
     Psalm 85:9, *"...Salvation is nigh them that fear him;"*

2. **Negative Fear**

   Negative fear is faith in the devil. This fear is not of God. The first appearance of negative fear in the human race came after Adam and Eve sinned. Genesis 3:10, *"I heard thy voice in the garden, and I was afraid."* Revelation 21:8, *"But the fearful, and unbelieving ...shall have their part in the lake which burneth with fire and brimstone."*

   This kind of fear is like a dark shadow that envelopes you and imprisons your mind. At one time or another you have been a prisoner of fear.

Maybe it was fear of rejection, fear of uncertainty, fear of sickness, fear of death, fear of heights, fire, or water. Maybe it is the fear of dark or enclosed places. This kind of fear will choke out faith, joy, peace, love, and all good things. It binds, paralyzes, and weakens Christians as well as softens them up for the arrival of other bad spirits. This fear is having faith in the devil. Even Job understood he allowed the door of satanic oppression to be opened through fear.

Fear is:
False
Evidence
Appearing
Real

"For the thing which I greatly feared is come upon me, and that which I was afraid of is come unto me." Job 3:25

If you think on bad or negative things long enough, the devil can cause them to take place in your life. In the same way, God brings things to pass in your life when you have faith in Him.

Characteristics of a Spirit of Fear

- Phobias - fear of water, heights, fire, dark places, and enclosed places. Isaiah 13:7-8
- Torment, Isaiah 54:14; 1 John 4:18
- Nightmares, Psalms 91:5-6
- Fear of Man, Proverbs 29:25
- Anxiety or worry, 1 Peter 5:7
- Doubt, Matthew 8:26
- Fear of death, Psalms 55:4; Hebrews 2:15
- Heart attacks or heart problems, Luke 21:26
- Sarcasm, Proverbs 26:18-19
- Shyness, 1 Timothy 1:7
- Intimidation, Nehemiah 6:13
- Fear of sickness, Job 3:25
- Lack of commitment, 1 Timothy 5:12
- Feelings of inadequacy, Romans 8:15
- Critical people, Matthew 10:28
- Perfectionists, 2 Samuel 22:31
- Controlling other people, Romans 8:31
- Insecurity, Deuteronomy 31:16
- Sabotaging relationships, Proverbs 16:7
- Recluses, Nahum 1:7

How to Assassinate the Assassin of Fear

Fear was introduced to mankind through sin, so to get rid of fear, you must get right with God, and do these three things.

1. Discern Your Fear

Discern your fear by identifying, recognizing, detecting, or perceiving. 1 John 4:1, *"Beloved, believe not every spirit, but try the spirits whether they are of God: because many false prophets are gone out into the world."*

2. Disown Your Fear

To disown is to deliberately renounce or refuse to accept. Matthew 12:29-30 states, *"Or else how can one enter into a strong man's house, and spoil his goods, except he first bind the strong man? and then he will spoil his house. He that is not with me is against me; and he that gathereth not with me scattereth abroad."*

You allowed it in, either intentionally or unintentionally, and you must command it to go.

> Matthew 16:17-19, *"And Jesus answered and said unto him, Blessed art thou, Simon Barjona: for flesh and blood hath not revealed it unto thee, but my Father which is in heaven.*

And I say also unto thee, That thou art Peter, and upon this rock I will build my church; and the gates of hell shall not prevail against it.

And I will give unto thee the keys of the kingdom of heaven: and whatsoever thou shalt bind on earth shall be bound in heaven: and whatsoever thou shalt loose on earth shall be loosed in heaven."

3. Displace Your Fear

To displace is to remove something old and replace it with something new. Matthew 12:43-45, *"When an unclean spirit is gone out of a man, it goes through arid places seeking rest and does not find it. Then it says, "I will return to the house I left." When it arrives, it finds the house unoccupied, swept clean and put in order. Then it goes and takes with it seven other spirits more wicked than itself, and they go in and live there. And the final condition of that man is worse than the first."*

That is how it will be with this wicked generation. If your house is left empty, it is an open invitation for worse trouble. Your house must be emptied of evil and filled with good.

The only way to move out of fear is to move in to love. Love is what must be loosed in order to overcome fear. You must love yourself, others, God, and allow yourself to be loved by others and by God.

> ***Security in life comes through giving to others.***

"There is no fear in love; but perfect love casteth out fear: because fear hath torment. He that feareth is not made perfect in love."
1 John 4:18

Security in life comes through giving to others. It's not what people do for you, but what you do for them that determines security in your heart.

Bind: Spirit of Fear
Loose: Spirit of Love
Read: 2 Timothy 1:7; Psalm 55:22; Deuteronomy 31:6

SPIRIT OF ERROR
1 John 4:6

"We are of God: he that knoweth God heareth us; he that is not of God heareth not us. Hereby know we the spirit of truth, and the spirit of error."

The Spirit of Error believes and spreads falsehoods. John warns that people who teach the truth won't win any popularity contests, because people don't want to hear that they need to change their behavior. False teachers are popular with the world because they tell people what they want to hear. That is one way for us to know who the true Christians are: by whether they want the truth or not. Many people get bad teaching that leads them, unintentionally, into believing something that is not true. This Spirit of Error operates best when there is an ignorance of God's Word. People who are dominated by this strongman cannot see their error; if they could, they would stop. Their minds become so clouded by this strongman that they are absolutely convinced they are right, and everyone else is wrong. Some examples include:

- Some people once thought you had to wear green in order for God to move.
- Some people left a city because they thought the power of the devil was so strong after God had sent them.

- Some believe you must speak in tongues to get to Heaven.
- Some people say you don't need to go to church to be saved.

Truth Can Be:
- **Distorted,** Acts 20:25-31
- **Suppressed,** Romans 1:18-20
- **Rejected,** Romans 2:5-11
- **Refused,** 2 Thessalonians 2:10
- **Denied,** 2 Thessalonians 2:12
- **Chosen,** 1 John 1:5-10

Truth is important to people who want more of God and to those who want to be led by the Holy Spirit. On Jesus' last night with His disciples, He promised He would send the Holy Spirit. Three times on that last night Jesus referred to the Holy Spirit as the Spirit of Truth.

> *"And I will pray the Father, and he shall give you another Comforter, that he may abide with you forever; Even the Spirit of truth; whom the world cannot receive, because it sees him not, neither knoweth him; but ye know him, for he dwelleth with you and shall be in you."* John 14:16, 17

> *"But when the Comforter is come, whom I will send unto you from the Father, even the Spirit of truth, which proceedeth from the Father, he shall testify of me: and ye also shall bear witness,*

because ye have been with me from the beginning. John 15:26-27

"Howbeit when he, the Spirit of truth, is come, he will guide you into all truth: for he shall not speak of himself; but whatsoever he shall hear, that shall he speak: and he will show you things to come. He shall glorify me: for he shall receive of mine, and shall shew it unto you." John 16:13-14

If you want to be led by the Holy Spirit, you must seek and accept the truth whether you like it or not. The knowledge of the truth will set you free. John 8:32

Characteristics of a Spirit of Error

- Unteachable, Proverbs 10:17
- Unsubmissive, Proverbs 29:1
- False religions, teachers, and prophets, 1 Timothy 6:20-21
- Can't admit wrongs
- Stubborn
- Defensive
- Argumentative
- Unstable
- Wrong belief system
- Makes assumptions

The mind is a battleground where the devil wages war upon the saints of God. He wants to get you to assume, believe or think something is true when it isn't. The devil knows whatever you believe in your mind, whether it is true or not, will control your life. The Bible tells us in Proverbs 23:7, *"For he thinketh in his heart, so is he."* That is why the Lord wants you to take into captivity every single thought to the obedience of Christ. If you allow the enemy to fill your mind with junk, he will gain the advantage and will create a stronghold in your life.

Four Assumptions from the Enemy

1. **Don't Assume Your Problems do not Have Solutions**
   In John 6:5-13, Philip assessed the cost of the problem and assumed no solution was possible. We can limit what God can do by assuming what is not possible.

2. **Don't Assume You Married the Wrong Person**
   In 1 Corinthians 7:17-24, the Corinthians thought after salvation they could get a new spouse. The devil tried to convince people they married the wrong person. Paul was telling them when you get saved, be a Christian where you're at. Don't change jobs unless it is immoral or unethical, and don't seek a divorce just because of salvation.

3. **Don't Assume the Worst in Other People**

   In Deuteronomy 13:12-15, God established a principle, so people would not act on a rumor and start a war. God was telling them that there are two sides to a story, so check out the facts before taking action. The devil wants you to believe talking to a person won't do any good. Someone once said there are two sides to every story, and then there is the truth. In Numbers 32, representatives of these three tribes didn't explain themselves clearly, and because of that, Moses jumped to conclusions and assumed they had selfish motives trying to avoid helping fight for the Promised Land. In reality, they were willing to fight, but they were just looking for safety for their wives and children.

   In Joshua 22:11-34, these three tribes built an altar at the Jordan River. Joshua thought they were starting their own religion, and they were ready to start a war. But, they followed this principle and avoided war. Instead of assuming, they went to ask. The altar was built to the same God who gave them victory. One of the hardest things to do is to believe your enemies can change.

4. **Don't Assume Someone Won't Respond to the Gospel**

   Acts 9:10-22; Do not allow the enemy to convince you not to share the Gospel with someone for fear that they will reject you. It is your job to plant the seed regardless if they respond to it positively or not. Do your job by planting the seed, and then believe God overtime to reap the harvest of salvation.

How to Assassinate the Assassin of a Spirit of Error

1. **Comprehend the Truth**
2. **Conform to the Truth**
3. **Communicate the Truth**

Bind: Spirit of Error
Loose: Spirit of Truth
Read: John 8:32

THE CRITICAL SPIRIT
Isaiah 58:9

"Then shalt thou call, and the Lord shall answer; thou shalt cry, and he shall say, Here I am. If thou take away from the midst of thee the yoke, the putting forth of the finger, and speaking vanity;"

A conscientious wife tried hard to please her critical husband but failed regularly. He was the most cantankerous at breakfast. If she prepared scrambled eggs, he wanted poached; if poached eggs, he wanted scrambled. One morning the wife poached one egg and scrambled the other and placed the plate before him. Anxiously she waited what surely this time would be his unqualified approval. He peered down at the plate and snorted, "Can't you do anything right, woman? You've scrambled the wrong one!"

If it isn't Good, Honest, or Loving, DO NOT say it!!

A critic is someone who points out how imperfectly other people do what the critic doesn't do at all. According to Isaiah 58:8-9, a critical spirit will keep the ears of God away from your voice.

There are two ministries that go on continually before God's throne:

1. **Ministry of Intercession,** Hebrews 7:25; Jesus is praying for us.

2. **Ministry of Accusation,** Revelation 12:10; Satan is always accusing us.

The person with a critical spirit is usually critical of everyone except themselves. They're so busy looking for the specks in other people's eyes, they can't see the plank, or "2x4", in their own eyes. The thing you must remember is that when you criticize people, you really criticize God. Let me ask you a question, "When you criticize someone's child, who takes offense?" Is it not the parents? God takes offense when you criticize and judge other people because He is their Father.

"Judge not, that ye be not judged."
Matthew 7:1

"For if we judge ourselves, we should not be judged." 1 Corinthians 11:31

Characteristics of a Critical Spirit

- Judges others
- Jealous
- Suspicious
- Prideful
- Opinionated
- Fault finders

- Gossipers
- Rejects those who are different
- Negative
- Mind and thoughts rule them

Five Ways to Know When I am Judging

1. A Person's Failure Improves the Opinion I have of Myself
2. A Person's Failure Decreases My Concerns for My Faults
3. A Person's Failure Causes Me to Seek Judgment in the Form of Punishment
4. A Person's Failure Causes Me to Feel that I Cannot Forgive
5. A Person's Failure Causes Me to Review Their Past Failures

How to Assassinate an Assassin of a Critical Spirit
Revelation 12:11

1. Blood of the Lamb
2. Word of Our Testimony
3. By Selfless Dedication unto God

Bind: A Critical Spirit
Loose: Positive Thoughts and Words
Read: Philippians 4:8

SPIRIT OF INFIRMITY
John 5:2-8

"Now there is at Jerusalem by the sheep market a pool, which is called in the Hebrew tongue Bethesda, having five porches. In these lay a great multitude of impotent folk, of blind, halt, withered, waiting for the moving of the water. For an angel went down at a certain season into the pool, and troubled the water: whosoever then first after the troubling of the water stepped in was made whole of whatsoever disease he had. And a certain man was there, which had an infirmity thirty and eight years. When Jesus saw him lie, and knew that he had been now a long time in that case, he saith unto him, Wilt thou be made whole? The impotent man answered him, Sir, I have no man, when the water is troubled, to put me into the pool: but while I am coming, another steppeth down before me. Jesus saith unto him, Rise, take up thy bed, and walk."

An infirmity is a physical weakness or defect. For 38 years, this man laid by a place that could have provided his healing. Yet, every time the waters were stirred and healing was made available, he watched others who were, maybe less sick, but more desperate, receive their healing. But, one day Jesus came and asked, "Do you want to get well?", and He healed him. My question to you is, "Do you want to get well?" According to Acts 10:34, God is no respecter of persons and what He has done for one, He can do for all. Just as the fall of man (Adam) introduced sickness as part of the curse, the Cross of Christ has introduced healing as part of the cure.

Paul summed up Jesus' ministry in Acts 10:38 - The blood of Jesus has broken satan's legal hold on your life. If you buy something, you get a receipt. God's receipt for us is the blood of Jesus.

Characteristics of a Spirit of Infirmity

- Colds, Matthew 5:5
- Fevers, Matthew 5:5
- Viral infections, Matthew 5:5
- Asthma, Matthew 5:5
- Arthritis, Matthew 5:5
- Fungus and warts, Matthew 5:5
- Hunchback, Luke 13:11
- Hay fever, Matthew 5:5
- Female problems, Matthew 9:20
- Tumors, 2 Timothy 2:17
- Sinus problems, Matthew 5:5
- Ear aches, Matthew 5:5
- Cancer, 2 Timothy 2:17
- Lumps on breasts, Matthew 9:20
- Cysts, Matthew 9:20
- Irregular periods, Matthew 9:20

Examples of Healing From a Spirit of Infirmity

- Mary Magdalene was not only healed of demonic bondage, but also of a Spirit of Infirmity, Luke 8:2.
- An unknown woman in Luke 13:10-13 was healed of a Spirit of Infirmity that had been in her for 18 years.
- The highest ranking Roman official on the island of Malta was Publius. His father was healed of a Spirit of Infirmity after Paul laid his hands on him in Acts 28:8.

Persistent faith is the key to unlocking healing.

Three Facts about Healing

1. **It is the Will of God to Heal,** Mark 1:40-45.
2. **Healings are Signs and Wonders,** Romans 15:18-19. Signs and wonders come as a result of obedience, and greater obedience comes as a result of signs and wonders
3. **Persistent Faith is the Key to Unlocking Healing,** Mark 5:24-34.

How to Assassinate the Assassin of Infirmity

1. **Anointing with Oil,** James 5:14-15
2. **Laying on of Hands,** Mark 16:17-18
3. **Prayer of Faith**, Mark 11:24
4. **Agreement,** Matthew 18:19-20
5. **Anointed Cloths** (prayer cloths), Acts 19:12
6. **Through a Prophetic Word,** 2 Kings 5:9-15

Bind: A Spirit of Infirmity
Loose: Healing and Health
Read: Isaiah 53:5

CHAPTER

SPIRITUAL ASSASSINS II

THE SPIRIT OF ANTICHRIST
1 John 2:18

"And every spirit that confesseth not that Jesus Christ is come in the flesh is not of God: and this is that Spirit of Antichrist, whereof ye have heard that it should come; and even now already is it in the world."
1 John 4:3

The Antichrist is anything anti, or against, Christ; to oppose or be against His teachings, a False Christ

Characteristics of an Antichrist Spirit

- They are against Christ
- They attempt to take the place of Christ
- They oppose Jesus' doctrine, deity, and resurrection, 1 John 2:22
- They believe in other methods of forgiveness of sins
- They attack an individual's testimony as to what

the blood of Christ has done
- They speak against the gifts of the Spirit saying they are of Satan
- They suppress, irritate, harass, and disturb churches, fellowships, and ministries
- They persecute the saints
- They try to seduce the saints into error, 1 Timothy 4:1-4

Dealing with an Antichrist Spirit
2 John 7-11 (amp)

"For many deceivers [heretics, posing as Christians] have gone out into the world, those who do not acknowledge and confess the coming of Jesus Christ in the flesh (bodily form). This [person, the kind who does this] is the deceiver and the antichrist [that is, the antagonist of Christ].
Watch yourselves, so that you do not lose what we have accomplished together, but that you may receive a full and perfect reward [when He grants rewards to faithful believers].
Anyone who runs on ahead and does not remain in the doctrine of Christ [that is, one who is not content with what He taught], does not have God; but the one who continues to remain in the teaching [of Christ does have God], he has both the Father and the Son.
If anyone comes to you and does not bring this teaching [but diminishes or adds to the doctrine of Christ], do not receive or welcome him into your house, and do not give him a greeting or any encouragement;

for the one who gives him a greeting [who encourages him or wishes him success, unwittingly] participates in his evil deeds."

How to Assassinate the Assassin of an Antichrist Spirit

1. **Focus on the Goodness of God**
2. **Remember the Victories of the Past**
3. **Be Positive in Your Speech**
4. **Do not Grow Weary in Well-doing**
5. **Use the Word of God to Dictate all Decisions**
6. **Pray Against Demonic Strongholds**
7. **Rebuke Deception**
8. **Be Content**
9. **Be Diligent in Pursuing the Lord**
10. **Guard Your Fellowship with Others**

Bind: Spirit of Antichrist
Loose: Testimonies of Blessings
Read: Romans 2:4

SPIRIT OF PERVERSION
Isaiah 19:14

"The Lord hath mingled a perverse spirit in the midst thereof: and they have caused Egypt to err in every work thereof: as a drunken man staggereth in his vomit..."

"Know ye not that the unrighteous shall not inherit the kingdom of God? Be not deceived: neither fornicators, nor idolaters, nor adulterers, nor effeminate, nor abusers of themselves with mankind, Nor thieves, nor covetous, nor drunkards, nor revilers, nor extortioners, shall inherit the kingdom of God. And such were some of you: but ye are washed, but ye are sanctified, but ye are justified in the name of the Lord Jesus, and by the Spirit of our God." 1 Corinthians 6:9-11

Romans 1:17-32 is a description of people who have submitted to a perverse spirit. It was only when Adam and Eve sinned that people became self-conscious about themselves and begin to judge others on their outward appearance.

Characteristics of a Perverse Spirit

- Lust, Proverbs 23:33
- Homosexuality
- Prostitution
- Abortion, Exodus 21:22-25, Exodus 20:13
- Incest
- Pornography
- Child Abuse
- Fornication
- Masturbation
- Adultery
- Bestiality
- Perverse speech: dirty jokes, cussing, gossiping, and bad mouthing others

These sins were punishable by death in the Old Testament:

"And the man that committeth adultery with another man's wife, even he that committeth adultery with his neighbour's wife, the adulterer and the adulteress shall surely be put to death.
And the man that lieth with his father's wife hath uncovered his father's nakedness: both of them shall surely be put to death; their blood shall be upon them.

And if a man lie with his daughter in law, both of them shall surely be put to death: they have wrought confusion; their blood shall be upon them.

If a man also lie with mankind, as he lieth with a woman, both of them have committed an abomination: they shall surely be put to death; their blood shall be upon them.

And if a man take a wife and her mother, it is wickedness: they shall be burnt with fire, both he and they; that there be no wickedness among you.

And if a man lie with a beast, he shall surely be put to death: and ye shall slay the beast.

And if a woman approach unto any beast, and lie down thereto, thou shalt kill the woman, and the beast: they shall surely be put to death; their blood shall be upon them.

And if a man shall take his sister, his father's daughter, or his mother's daughter, and see her nakedness, and she see his nakedness; it is a wicked thing; and they shall be cut off in the sight of their people: he hath uncovered his sister's nakedness; he shall bear his iniquity." Lev. 20:10-17

Soul Ties

Sexual sins create bad soul ties. Soul ties are emotional and spiritual "love bonds" that connect and draw people together. Soul ties are formed when two people become bonded together or become one. They can be good or evil, holy or profane. Here are some different kinds of soul ties or "love bonds".

- **Marriage Soul Ties,** Ephesians 5:31; Mt 19:6
- **Friendship Soul Ties,** 1 Samuel 18:1
- **Parent/Child Soul Ties,** Genesis 44:30,31
- **Christian Soul Ties**, Ephesians 4:16
- **Sexual Soul Ties,** 1 Corinthians 6:16
  Inappropriate affections, immoral fantasies, and sexual relations outside of marriage form sexual soul ties.

Know this; temptation will come. But it is not beyond your ability to overcome it. God will make a way out.

> *"No temptation has overtaken you except what is common to mankind. And God is faithful; he will not let you be tempted beyond what you can bear. But when you are tempted, he will also provide a way out so that you can endure it."* 1 Corinthians 10:13

The best way to avoid soul ties is to avoid getting into bad situations before they happen. Decide now to remain pure and not wait till the moment of weakness. Always remember desire plus opportunity equals sin. If you have the opportunity, pray against desire. If you have desire, pray against opportunities. The following "10 Commandments" will help you avoid bad soul ties.

How to Assassinate the Assassin of Perversion

10 Sexual Commandments to Deliverance

I. Thou shall not counsel the opposite sex alone.

II. Thou shall not pray with the opposite sex until marriage.

III. Thou shall be careful in talking with or writing to the opposite sex.

IV. Thou shall not discuss marriage problems with the opposite sex.

V. Thou shall not show improper affection toward the opposite sex.

VI. Thou shall not engage in immoral fantasies or pornography.

VII. Thou shall make an oath of purity to be faithful to the Lord.

VIII. Thou shall not pursue unhealthy and immoral means of sexual gratification.

IX. Thou shall not self-satisfy thy sexual desires.

X. Thou shall avoid the lust of the flesh.

Bind: A Perverse Spirit
Loose: Ability to Resist Temptation
Read: 2 Corinthians 10:5

LYING SPIRIT
Isaiah 59:1-5

"Behold, the Lord's hand is not shortened, that it cannot save; neither his ear heavy, that it cannot hear: But your iniquities have separated between you and your God, and your sins have hid his face from you, that he will not hear. For your hands are defiled with blood, and your fingers with iniquity; your lips have spoken lies, your tongue hath muttered perverseness. None calleth for justice, nor any pleadeth for truth: they trust in vanity, and speak lies; they conceive mischief, and bring forth iniquity. They hatch cockatrice' eggs, and weave the spider's web: he that eateth of their eggs dieth, and that which is crushed breaketh out into a viper."

Sin not only offends God, but it separates us from the presence of God. Because God is holy, He cannot ignore, excuse, or tolerate sin. Sin forms a wall that isolates us from the presence of God. One of the most detestable sins to God is lying. Two reasons He hates lying so much is:

1. **Lying is Contrary to His Holy Nature**
   In John 14:6, Jesus said, *"...I am the way, the truth, and the life..."*

2. **Lying is Complimentary to the Nature of the Devil**

   In John 8:44, Jesus called the devil the *"father of lies."*

Three Kinds of Liars

1. **Liars by Intention**

   An intentional lie is a lie without an excuse. Habitual liars, excuse makers, and exaggerators are forms of intentional liars.

2. **Liars by Insinuation**

   Not all lying is done by words. Insinuation is to imply something so that someone concludes an untruth. Example: "You don't know them like I do."

3. **Liars by Incompletion**

   An incomplete liar is one who tells only half the truth. This leaves a false impression when the whole truth would explain the matter.

When we talk about a lying spirit, we refer to those who tell lies and those who believe lies.

Sin forms a wall that isolates us from the presence of God.

Characteristics of a Lying Spirit

- Flattery - Proverbs says: *"a flattering mouth worketh ruin."* and the *"Wounds of a friend are better than kisses from an enemy."*

    In 1 Thessalonians 2:5, Paul told the Thessalonians he never used flattery to get bigger offerings.

    If you give compliments to get something, or if you are given a compliment and you become gullible, you need prayer for being manipulated by a lying spirit.

- Deception - *"Even him, whose coming is after the working of Satan with all power and signs and lying wonders, And with all deceivableness of unrighteousness in them that perish; because they received not the love of the truth, that they might be saved."* 2 Thessalonians 2:9-10

- Slanderers - *"He that hideth hatred with lying lips, and he that uttereth a slander, is a fool."* Proverbs 10:18

- False Teachers - *"O Timothy, keep that which is committed to thy trust, avoiding profane and vain babblings, and oppositions of science falsely so called:"* 1 Timothy 6:20

- Accusers - *"Let the lying lips be put to silence;*

which speak grievous things proudly and contemptuously against the righteous." Psalms 31:18

- Exaggerators - *"What this adds up to, then, is this: no more lies, no more pretense. Tell your neighbor the truth. In Christ's body we're all connected to each other, after all. When you lie to others, you end up lying to yourself."* Ephesians 4:25 (MSG)

- Gossipers - *"He that goeth about as a talebearer revealeth secrets: therefore meddle not with him that flattereth with his lips.* Proverbs 20:19

    "But shun profane and vain babblings: for they will increase unto more ungodliness." 2 Timothy 2:16

- Superstitious - *"But refuse profane and old wives fables, and exercise thyself rather unto godliness."* 1 Timothy 4:7

    Examples: black cats bring bad luck, broken mirrors, walking under a ladder, wearing pendants to ward off evil, or belief in the Tooth Fairy, Easter Bunny, or Santa Claus.

- Hypocrites - Psalm 78:36, *"Nevertheless they did flatter him with their mouth, and they lied unto him with their tongues."*
Hypocrite = actor, religious spirit

How to Assassinate the Assassin of a Lying Spirit

1. **Love the Truth,** 2 Thessalonians 2:10
   A person is not a liar because he tells lies, He tells lies because he is a liar. You have to love the truth to change, not just hate lying.

2. **Learn the Truth**, Philippians 4:8
   Saturate your mind with the truth. It's natural to lie, that is why you need to live in the supernatural.

3. **Live the Truth**, Ephesians 4:25
   Be open to others stopping you when you gossip and slander. Be accountable.

Bind: A Lying Spirit
Loose: A Spirit of Truth
Read: John 8:32

SPIRIT OF SLUMBER
Proverbs 6:6

"Go to the ant, thou sluggard: consider her ways, and be wise."

Slumber is an inactive state. Some people are under the false impression that work is a curse. Before sin ever entered the human race, Adam was assigned the task of cultivating the Garden of Eden (Genesis 2:15). The curse that followed the fall had to do with hassles and irritations that accompany work, not work itself. Work is a privilege, a challenge, an answer to boredom, and a place to invest one's energy, not to mention a way to provide for your needs. Throughout the Bible we are encouraged to be diligent, and committed, to tasks in life that need to be accomplished.

Characteristics of a Spirit of Slumber/Sluggard

A Sluggard is a lazy person.

- The Sluggard has No Motivation
  "How long wilt thou sleep, O sluggard? when wilt thou arise out of thy sleep? Yet a little sleep, a little slumber, a little folding of the hands to sleep: So shall thy poverty come as one that traveleth, and thy want as an armed man." Proverbs 6:9-11

- The Sluggard is a Quitter
  "The sluggard will not plow by reason of the cold; therefore shall he beg in harvest, and have nothing." Proverbs 20:4. They want to reap what they haven't plowed or planted.

- The Sluggard is Unfulfilled
  "The soul of the sluggard desireth, and hath nothing: but the soul of the diligent shall be made fat." Proverbs 13:4

  "The desire of the slothful killeth him; for his hands refuse to labour. He covetheth greedily all the day long: but the righteous giveth and spareth not." Proverbs 21:25-26

  Vision, Strategy and organization go together:
  - Vision = Where you want to go.
  - Strategy = How to get there.
  - Organization = The people used to get there.

- The Sluggard Takes a Toll on Others
  "He also that is slothful in his work is brother to him that is a great waster." Proverbs 18:9

- The Sluggard Lives by Excuses
  "The slothful man saith, There is a lion without, I shall be slain in the streets." Proverbs 22:13

  "The slothful man saith, There is a lion in the way; a lion is in the streets. As the door turneth

upon his hinges, so doth the slothful upon his bed. The slothful hideth his hand in his bosom; it grieveth him to bring it again to his mouth." Proverbs 26:13-15

- The Sluggard is Defensive
  "The sluggard is wiser in his own conceit than seven men that can render a reason." Proverbs 26:16

> **Jesus came to serve, not to be served.**

Involvement is the only way to break the Spirit of Slumber. It is important that we incorporate all three of the following Biblical commands for spiritual involvement.

How to Assassinate the Assassin of Slumber

We need to be busy about the Lord's work. There are three phases of involvement to break a spirit of slumber.

1. **The Great Commandment,** 1 Corinthians 13
   The Great Commandment is to *love others*. W*ithout love we have nothing*, 1 Corinthians 13:2

2. **The Great Commission,** Acts 1:18
   The Great Commission is to *witness to others*. We need to be a witness of what we have seen and heard.

3. **The Great Commitment,** Ephesians 6:7-8
   The Great Commitment is to *serve others*. Jesus came not to be served, but to serve. Instead of looking to get blessed, look for someone you can be a blessing to.

Bind: A Spirit of Slumber
Loose: A Spirit to Work
Read: Galatians 6:9

SPIRIT OF DIVINATION
Acts 16:16-18

"And it came to pass, as we went to prayer, a certain damsel possessed with a spirit of divination met us, which brought her masters much gain by soothsaying: The same followed Paul and us, and cried, saying, These men are the servants of the most high God, which shew unto us the way of salvation. And this did she many days. But Paul, being grieved, turned and said to the spirit, I command thee in the name of Jesus Christ to come out of her. And he came out the same hour."

Why was Paul annoyed at the truthful words from the demon? Because truth and evil don't mix. If Paul accepted those words from the demon, he would link the Gospel with demon related activities. Demons will try to make others believe and insinuate they are working closely with good ministers.

Divination is the practice of attempting to foretell future events, or discover hidden knowledge, by occult or supernatural means. This spirit is growing quickly. Here are some scary statistics regarding things of a spirit of divination:

1. A 2005 Gallup Poll revealed that 3 in 4 Americans believe in the paranormal.

2. The American Religious Identification Survey gave Wicca an average annual growth of 143% for the period 1990 to 2001 (from 8,000 to 134,000 – U.S. data / similar for Canada and Australia). According to The Statesman Anne Elizabeth Wynn claims "The two most recent American Religious Identification Surveys declare Wicca, one form of paganism, as the fastest growing spiritual identification in America."

3. According to a 2006 Associated Press poll, 32 million people believe in astrology, and one in four reads their horoscope regularly, letting it run their lives.

Why is going to psychics or reading horoscopes wrong?

- Jeremiah 27 - God hates it because it leads people to seek satanic intelligence for guidance rather than God and His Word. He didn't create this world to have His children go to the creation, instead of The Creator, for guidance.
- Leviticus 20:6 & 27 - Consulting mediums and letting your life be ruled by the stars or psychics was a crime with a penalty of death.
- Revelation 21:8 - Sorcerers are listed with murders, liars, and idolaters as those who will have a place in the lake, which burneth with fire and brimstone.

- Galatians 5:20 - Witchcraft is listed as a work of the flesh.

    "Be ye not unequally yoked together with unbelievers: for what fellowship hath righteousness with unrighteousness? and what communion hath light with darkness? And what concord hath Christ with Belial? or what part hath he that believeth with an infidel? And what agreement hath the temple of God with idols? for ye are the temple of the living God; as God hath said, I will dwell in them, and walk in them; and I will be their God, and they shall be my people. Wherefore come out from among them, and be ye separate, saith the Lord, and touch not the unclean thing; and I will receive you. And will be a Father unto you, and ye shall be my sons and daughters, saith the Lord Almighty" 2 Corinthians 6:14-18.

The way God's people receive divine revelation is by the Holy Spirit; fortune tellers receive information from demonic spirits.

Characteristics of a Spirit of Divination

- Fortune telling - Micah 5:12, *"...and you shall have no more tellers of fortunes;"* (ESV)

- Horoscopes - Leviticus 19:26, *"Do not practice divination or sorcery."*(MSG) Demonic spirits cannot be relied upon for guidance. They mix their limited knowledge with lies to get people's attention.
- Ouija Board - a board with the alphabet on it and a planchette (triangular piece of wood on rollers) that is used to spell out supernatural messages. There were two young kids playing with the Ouija board, and they asked about the power behind the board. "Who are you?", they asked. Two times the response was, "You know who I am." The third time the response was, "Go to Hell."
- Magic - whether black or white magic. Black magic produces curses, and white magic removes curses. Either way, a magician tries to compel an evil spirit to work for him.
- Hypnosis - There are infomercials about how hypnosis helped people stop drinking, smoking, lose weight and sleep at night.
- Drugs - Revelation 21:8; 22:15. The Greek word for sorcery is *pharmakos* which means drugs; illegal or legal prescription drugs.

Judge them by their fruits, not their suits.

Don't be addicted.
- Handwriting Analysis - to take a handwriting sample and predict the future.
- Palm reading - Leviticus 19:31, *"Do not turn to mediums or necromancers;"*(ESV)
- Souvenirs, Idols, and Statues - some factories allow witch doctors to pronounce incantations over items that we buy and bring into our homes.
- Voyeurism or Peeping Tom - one who gets pleasure from watching others from a place of concealment, Matthew 5:27-28.
- Games, Table Games, Video Games, and Card Games - teaching our kids to cast spells.
- Cartoons and Toys - i.e. magic 8 ball, 1 Corinthians 15:33
- Necromancer - Leviticus 19:31, *"Do not turn to mediums or necromancers;"* (ESV). It is one who consults the dead.
- Rebellion - I Samuel 15:23, *"For rebellion is as the sin of witchcraft..."* Rebellion grows out of a negative attitude.

How to Assassinate an Assassin of Divination

- **Judge all Spirits**
- **Engage in Godly Discernment**

- **Don't be Impressed by all Manifestations**
- **Don't be Deceived by Partial Truth**
- **Guard Your Feelings, Emotions, and Your Will Against Enticement**
- **Avoid Evil**
- **Hate Sin**
- **Pray for God's Light to Expose Darkness**
- **Don't be Drawn Away and Enticed to Participate in Demonic Activities**

Bind: A Spirit of Divination
Loose: Whole Armor of God
Read: Deuteronomy 4:19

SPIRIT OF ISHMAEL
Galatians 4:21-31

"For it is written, that Abraham had two sons, the one by a bondmaid, the other by a freewoman. But he who was of the bondwoman was born after the flesh; but he of the freewoman was by promise." 4:22-23

There are two forces at work in the world today; God and the devil, and each are trying to build a team of people to extend their kingdom on earth.

- True bride of Christ, Revelation 12
- Harlot or false bride of Christ, Revelation 17

These scriptures in Galatians give us some characteristics between the true bride and the false bride of Christ. Just because people have a church and call themselves pastors or Christians, doesn't mean they are a true church. God uses an allegory, a story with a meaning beyond the literal, to teach us not to be part of the harlot/false church. It is a church that's creating Ishmael's or works of the flesh. Instead, we need to be a part of a true church that is being led by the Spirit of God.

Hagar
- Bondwoman
- Has Son, Ismael (bond son)

Sarah
- Free woman
- Has Son, Isaac (free son)

- Has a son born of the flesh
- Son is a product of man's work
- Has a son born of the Spirit
- Son is a product of faith, God's work

There are two types of Ishmaels:
- Ishmael churches
- Personal Ishmaels

An Ismael church is a place where the Glory of the Lord has departed. A personal Ishmael is a product of self-effort, impatience, or works of the flesh. It's a substitute for God's best. It's God's permissive will, not His perfect will.

Characteristics of Ishmael Church/People

- Bound, have a form of religion but deny the power
- Enjoy fleshly, worldly things more than things of God
- Man-pleasers; looking for the applause of man instead of the approval of God
- Persecute the true church
- Deceitful; willing to do anything to get what they want
- Twist God's Word to make it fit into their lives
- Sinning doesn't bother them
- Extremely impatient

- Desire to be right
- Loves to argue

How Assassinate the Assassin of an Ishmael Spirit

- **Do not Modify God's Original Instructions**
- **Do not Minimize Sins Impact**
- **Do not Manifest Fleshly Impatience,**
  It was 25 years from the promise of Isaac until his birth.

Some of the greatest failures of the greatest figures of the Bible resulted from their impatience with God as they waited for a prophecy to be fulfilled. Whenever you jump ahead of God's timetable, you always produce something in the flesh that opposes God's will for your life.

Bind: A Spirit of Ishmael
Loose: A Spirit of Legitimacy and Faithfulness
Read: Deuteronomy 10:12-13

SPIRIT OF KORAH
Numbers 16:1-40

"Now Korah, the son of Izhar, the son of Kohath, the son of Levi, and Dathan and Abiram, the sons of Eliab, and On, the son of Peleth, sons of Reuben, took men: And they rose up before Moses, with certain of the children of Israel, two hundred and fifty princes of the assembly, famous in the congregation, men of renown: And they gathered themselves together against Moses and against Aaron, and said unto them, Ye take too much upon you, seeing all the congregation are holy, every one of them, and the Lord is among them: wherefore then lift ye up yourselves above the congregation of the Lord?"

Korah was a very popular and influential person in Israel during the exodus from Egypt to the Promised Land. In Exodus 6, Korah was mentioned among the chief men of Israel. But, Korah began to be disgruntled with Moses and Aaron and instigated a rebellion by recruiting a grievance committee and confronting Moses and Aaron with their complaints. Korah did not like what the leaders were saying or doing and he began to make accusations like:

- You've not delegated enough power; you take too

much on yourself, v.3
- You think you're the only holy ones in the congregation, v.3
- You don't spend enough time with us. Korah wanted Aaron's position and was jealous of anyone who spent time with Moses, v. 13
- You don't keep your promises. The fulfillment of the promise was still to come, but it wasn't fast enough for them, v.14

A Spirit of Korah mostly attaches to men. But remember, spirits are not male or female; they are good or evil. A Spirit of Korah either attaches itself to leaders or is attracted to leaders. At first, people with a Spirit of Korah will appear friendly, charming, helpful, and supportive. But eventually their true motives will be revealed.

> **Bad company corrupts good morals.**

Four examples of Biblical characters that had a Spirit of Korah:

1. Jacob was a deceiver who stole from his own brother.

2. Judas betrayed Jesus for 30 pieces of silver.

3. Saul caused division, was jealous of David and attempted to kill him.

4. Lucifer was like "heaven's associate pastor" who led the first church split.

Characteristics of a Spirit of Korah

- Seeks to be popular
- Desires to have a title or position to feel important
- Loves power and control
- Needs to feel close to leadership
- Resents people who spend time with leaders
- When rejected, will retaliate even against close friends and loved ones
- Loves to argue
- Discontent
- Deceitful
- Jealous
- Hates submission
- Leads secret prayer meetings and Bible studies
- Sympathizes with doers of evil
- Preys on weak, young Christians to give counsel and instruction
- Greedy

- Disloyal
- Holds Grudges
- Selfish ambition
- Unhealthy desire to achieve something

How to Assassinate the Assassin of a Spirit of Korah

1. **Stay under Authority of Your Local Church and Pastor.** Romans 16:17-18.

2. **Ask Questions:**
   - Why do they want to be my friend?
   - Who am I when I am around them?
   - What kind of fruit are they bearing?
   - How many pastors have they had in the past 5 years?
   - Are they supporters of church and ministers?
   - When I am around them, what are our conversations about?

3. **Be Accountable to Those Over You in the Lord**

4. **Avoid Them**
   Bad company corrupts good morals. *"But now I have written unto you not to keep company, if any man that is called a brother be a fornicator, or covetous, or an idolator, or a railer, or a*

drunkard, or an extortioner; with such an one no not to eat. For what have I to do to judge them also that are without? do not ye judge them that are within?" 1 Corinthians 5:11-12.

Bind: A Critical Spirit and Rebellious Spirit
Loose: Ability to be Accountable to Leadership
Read: 1 Corinthians 4:2; Romans 13

SEDUCING SPIRITS
1 Timothy 4:1;
2 Thessalonians 2:9-12

> *"Now the Spirit speaketh expressly, that in the latter times some shall depart from the faith, giving heed to seducing spirits, and doctrines of devils;"* 1 Timothy 4:1

These spirits are especially active in the end-times. Their prime targets are believers of Christ, and their primary purpose is to get Christians to wander from the truth.

Seduce means to lure or attract in order to be lead astray; to persuade to be disobedient. Seducing spirits have a job, and that is to get your inward desires to respond, or connect, with outward enticement, so you will sin.

> *"But every man is tempted, when he is drawn away of his own lust, and enticed. Then when lust hath conceived, it bringeth forth sin: and sin, when it is finished, bringeth forth death."*
> James 1:14-15

This is the same tactic Satan used with Eve in the Garden of Eden. He dangled the temptation before her eyes in Genesis 3:6, and ultimately she responded to the temptation and committed sin.

Characteristics of a Seducing Spirit

- Selfishness
- Confusion
- Restless
- Curious
- Unrealistic
- Immature
- Deceitful
- Rebellious
- Unteachable
- Loves attention
- Lives in a fantasy world
- Unbalanced
- Lack of thought control
- Easily tempted
- Desires to please others
- Overly ambitious
- Desires to be famous

Basically you can sum up the seduction of mankind with these three general categories:

With Men	**With Women**
Gold	**Gold**
Girls	**Guys**
Glory	**Glory**

When it comes to overcoming a seducing spirit it is important to remember that this will be one of the most prevalent assassins of the last days.

Seven–Fold Desire of a Seducing Spirit

1. To Deceive You in Believing Lies
2. Lower the Spiritual Standard of the Word of God
3. Interfere with Your Spiritual Growth
4. Discourage Holiness
5. Pull You Away from Christ
6. Walk After the flesh
7. Question the Truth

Five Lies Seducing Spirits Tell You:

1. **Life Should be Easy**
   "In the sweat of thy face shalt thou eat bread, till thou return unto the ground; for out of it wast thou taken: for dust thou art, and unto dust shalt thou return." Genesis 3:19

2. **Life Should be Fair**
   "That ye may be the children of your Father which is in heaven: for he maketh his sun to rise on the evil and on the good, and sendeth rain on the just and on the unjust." Matthew 5:45

3. **God Doesn't Care About You and Your Problems**
   "Casting all your care upon him; for he careth for you." 1 Peter 5:7

4. **You Married the Wrong Person**
   "What therefore God has joined together, let not man separate." Mark 10:9 (ESV)

5. **If It Feels Good, Do It**
   "And be not conformed to this world: but be ye transformed by the renewing of your mind, that ye may prove what is that good, and acceptable, and perfect, will of God." Romans 12:2

How to Assassinate the Assassin of Seducing Spirits

1. **Stay Connected to Christ**
2. **Pray for Discernment**
3. **Judge all Decisions by the Word of God**
4. **Seek Counsel, and be Accountable to Leadership**
5. **Be Careful Who You Hang Out With**
6. **Love God, Not the World**

Bind: A Seducing Spirit
Loose: Spirit of Purity and Holiness
Read: 1 Corinthians 10:13

SPIRIT OF JEZEBEL
1 Kings 18 - 22

> *"And Ahab told Jezebel all that Elijah had done, and withal how he had slain all the prophets with the sword. Then Jezebel sent a messenger unto Elijah, saying, So let the gods do to me, and more also, if I make not thy life as the life of one of them by to morrow about this time."* 1 Kings 19:1-2

In 1 Kings 18-19, Jezebel was the wicked, rebellious, and Baal-worshipping wife of King Ahab, who was one of the most evil kings ever to reign.

> *"And Ahab the son of Omri did evil in the sight of the Lord above all that were before him. And it came to pass, as if it had been a light thing for him to walk in the sins of Jeroboam the son of Nebat, that he took to wife Jezebel the daughter of Ethbaal king of the Zidonians, and went and served Baal, and worshipped him. And he reared up an altar for Baal in the house of Baal, which he had built in Samaria. And Ahab made a grove; and Ahab did more to provoke the Lord God of Israel to anger than all the kings of Israel that were before him."*
> 1 Kings 16:30-33

Although she had no authority of her own, she desperately sought to be in control. She misused the king's throne and the spirit of this woman drove her to get whatever she wanted at any cost. She couldn't stand to be denied anything. She hated the prophets of God and wanted the people to serve Baal rather than Jehovah! In 2 Kings 9, she was thrown out of a window, trampled on by horses, and eaten by dogs to the point she was not recognizable. The same spirit that made her life miserable is roaming around trying to make friends with you. As a matter of fact, this spirit resurfaced in the church of Thyatira in Revelation 2:18-29.

> *A Jezebel Spirit seeks desperately to be in control.*

A Jezebel Spirit mostly attaches to women. Spirits are good or evil, not male or female; however, the spirit of rebellion has two branches:

- Spirit of Jezebel - mostly women
- Spirit Of Korah - mostly men

They have influential power to make threats that create fear and discouragement. It could be with people or demonic spirits. Even now, if you're doing all you can and things aren't going your way, it could be that someone with a Jezebel spirit is praying against you.

A Jezebel Spirit hates a Spirit of Elijah. It takes an Ahab to tolerate a Jezebel. People who have a spirit of Jezebel will have terrible marriages because the woman is always nagging, complaining, and is never happy with what she has. Ahab tolerates while Jezebel controls. At first, people with a Jezebel Spirit will appear friendly, charming, helpful, supportive, harmless, and loving. They do this to gain favor, make friends, and secure a position of influence to later bring destruction.

Characteristics of Jezebel Spirit

- They desire the upper hand
- They want to have the last word
- They have an excessive desire for power and control
- Self-centered
- Greedy
- Manipulative
- Easily offended
- Hold grudges
- Jealous
- Lie, connive, and cheat to get ahead
- They bring division
- Bad mouth husbands, bosses, and pastors
- Challenge authority
- Discontent
- Deceitful, 2 Kings 9:30; when Jehu was coming to kill her, she put on make-up, did her hair, and was

looking good
- They can't stand to be denied anything
- They make threats and/or manipulate others if they don't get their way
- They isolate themselves from some because they feel like they are better
- They hate the anointing and the anointed ones

How to Assassinate the Assassin of the Jezebel Spirit

1. **Stop Tolerating It**
2. **Set Boundaries, and Stick to Them**
3. **Disassociate Yourself from Others Moving in a Jezebel Sprit**
4. **Surround Yourself with the Right Kind of People,** 1 Kings 19:18
5. **Break the Word Curses off Your Life, so You are not Walking in Fear and Discouragement**
6. **Stay in the Presence of the Lord, and Walk in the Spirit**
7. **Pray for Those who are of a Jezebel Spirit**

Bind: A Spirit of Jezebel
Loose: A Spirit of Humility and Prayer
Read: Ephesians 4:2

CHAPTER 5

Spiritual Assassins III

Spirit of Ahithophel
2 Samuel 15:12

"And Absalom sent for Ahithophel the Gilonite, David's counsellor, from his city, even from Giloh, while he offered sacrifices. And the conspiracy was strong; for the people increased continually with Absalom."

The Spirit of Ahithophel can be simply defined as, "unforgiveness". Ahithophel was an extremely wise person. Even David considered Ahithophel's advice to be like getting counsel from God, 2 Samuel 16:23. We read in 1 Chronicles 27:33 that Ahithophel was the king's counselor.

As wise as Ahithophel was, he entered into some ungodly partnerships and allowed anger and unforgiveness to rule his heart. 2 Samuel 15 tells of the rebellion against David that was led by his own son, Absalom. Absalom was undermining David's authority for four years by kissing up to people and building relationships with others for his own personal advantage. As the days got closer for Absalom to actually overthrow his father from his kingly position, Absalom called Ahithophel to have a meeting. Remember, Ahithophel was a trusted advisor, even a cabinet member in the kingdom of David. Here, Absalom is reaching right into the heart of David's inner circle and attempting to have him join the rebellion. The Bible says that Ahithophel joined Absalom, and the conspiracy grew even stronger. Others began to think that if a wise man who counseled David, Ahithophel, had joined Absalom in this massive governmental overthrow, there had to be something going on with David that they didn't know, because even his closest confidants were now abandoning him and joining forces with Absalom. So, the question must be asked, "Why would this long time, trusted advisor turn on David and join forces with the enemy?" The answer is simple…unforgiveness.

Ahithophel had a son by the name of Eliam who was actually one of David's mighty men in 2 Samuel 23:34. Eliam had a daughter by the name of Bathsheba which also made her Ahithophel's granddaughter. In 2 Samuel 11, David saw this beautiful woman and inquired about her. David knew who she was and that she was married, but his lustful desires got the best of him; and, not only did he have sex with her, but Bathsheba became pregnant. In David's deep desire to hide his sin and be with Bathsheba, he also killed her husband, Uriah. Then, as you may recall in 2 Samuel 12, the judgment of God fell upon David when the son that was conceived between David and Bathsheba in their unholy union became ill and died. So, Ahithophel had his married granddaughter taken and her husband killed by David. He also lost a great grandson all because of David's inability to control his own fleshly desires. Ahithophel obviously quietly dealt with all these issues, while he faithfully served David, but there was still an underlying thread of unforgiveness that never got resolved. Absalom tapped into that unforgiveness and got Ahithophel to join forces with him.

It's very important to get healed of things, instead of just dealing with things, because sooner or later, it will surface to lead us astray. Forgiveness is essential to your spiritual health and advancement. Forgiveness is letting go of your desire for justice and offering grace to someone who has deeply offended you. It's not just important to know what

> *It's important to get healed of things instead of just dealing with things.*

forgiveness is, it's also important to know what forgiveness isn't.

Seven Truths about Forgiveness

1. **If I Forgive, I'm Not Saying What Happened That Hurt Me is "Okay".**
2. **Forgiveness is For Me, Not Just for the Offender.**
3. **Forgiveness Takes Strength. You Are Not a Weak Fool to Forgive.**
4. **Forgiveness Doesn't Give the Offender Permission to Hurt Me Again.**
5. **Forgiveness Often Takes Place When It's Still Painful, Not When All the Hurt Goes Away.**
6. **Forgiveness is an Act of Faith, Not a Feeling.**
7. **Forgiveness Doesn't Mean a Restored Relationship.**

The Spirit of Ahithophel is alive and well; unforgiveness is running rampant and will destroy everything and everyone in its path. Walk in forgiveness.

Characteristics of a Spirit of Ahithophel

- Unresolved offense
- Revenger seeker
- Holds things inside
- Unforgiveness

- Unholy alliances
- Easily persuaded
- Not good at confronting
- Bad communicator
- Good at giving advice but bad at personal application
- Smart but not wise
- Spontaneous
- Impatient
- Assumes
- Disloyal

How to Assassinate the Assassin of the Spirit of Ahithophel

The Spirit of Ahithophel is really a spirit of unforgiveness. In order to be delivered from unforgiveness, you must realize these three facts:

1. **Forgiveness is a Choice, not a Feeling.**
2. **When it Comes to Forgiveness, it Doesn't Matter "Who is Right" but "What is Right."**
3. **If You Don't Forgive Them, God Can't Forgive You.**

Bind: Unforgiveness
Loose: Forgiveness
Read: Colossians 3:13

SPIRIT OF REBELLION
1 Samuel 15:23

"For rebellion is as the sin of witchcraft, and stubbornness is as iniquity and idolatry. Because thou hast rejected the word of the Lord, he hath also rejected thee from being king."

Rebellion means to oppose, resist, or defy authority. Rebellion always grows out of a negative attitude.

The Path to Open Rebellion

- ➤ *Dissatisfaction*
- ➤ *Skepticism*
- ➤ *Complaining*
- ➤ *Resentment*
- ➤ *Bitterness*
- ➤ *Rebellion*

Characteristics of Rebellion

- Disobedient
- Defy authority

- Angry
- Unresolved issues
- Talk too much
- Lying
- Desire power and position
- Want followers
- Disruptive
- Stubborn
- Moody
- Resists good
- Witchcraft
- Unsubmissive
- Negative
- Rule-breaker
- Independent
- Think they are never wrong
- Don't like being told no
- Argumentative

Three Types of Rebellion

1. **Rebellion of Immaturity**
   In Numbers 14:1-4, Children murmur about their parents, or people complain against authority when they don't do what they want them to do.

2. **Rebellion of Familiarity**
   In Numbers 12:1-15, Miriam was mad at Moses for marrying a Cushite (black woman) and began

to rebel against his authority. God heard her bickering, punished her for a week with leprosy, and made her sit outside the camp. Familiarity breeds contempt.

3. **Rebellion of Pride**
In Numbers 16:1-16, Korah lead a rebellion against God's leaders.

How to Assassinate the Assassin of Rebellion

1. **Break the Power of Opposition off Your Life**
2. **Be More Agreeable**
3. **Repent of Your Last Act of Disobedience**
4. **Forgive Those Who have Hurt You and Let You Down**
5. **Be a Good Follower**
6. **Speak More Positive, and Find the Good in Others**
7. **Submit to Authority**
8. **Learn to Embrace Correction**
9. **Stop Complaining**

Bind: A Rebellious Spirit
Loose: A Greater Obedience to the Lord and compliance to His Word
Read: Isaiah 1:5; 31:6

FAMILIAR SPIRITS
1 Samuel 28:7-8

"Then said Saul unto his servants, Seek me a woman that hath a familiar spirit, that I man go to her, and enquire of her. And his servants said to him, behold, there is a woman that hath a familiar spirit at Endor. And Saul disguised himself, and put on other raiment, and he went, and two men with him, and they came to the woman by night; and he said, I pray thee, divine unto me by the familiar spirit, and bring me him up, who I shall name unto thee."

Familiar Spirits are in charge of passing down every evil trait, genetic disease, and an inheritance of unrepented sin to our children. Familiar Spirits will stay with a family until one of two things happen:

1. **Death to the Entire Lineage**
2. **Deliverance**

Characteristics of a Familiar Spirit

- Addictions
- Mental and emotional problems
- Physical infirmities
- Sexual sins

- Religious errors
- Speech problems - lying, cursing, criticizing, and gossiping

Familiar Spirits
Deuteronomy 7:1-6

Each of these families represent a familiar spirit.

1. **Hittites** = Fear
2. **Girgashites** = Compromise
3. **Amorites** = Pride
4. **Canaanites** = Materialism
5. **Perizzites** = Immorality
6. **Hivites** = Humanism
7. **Jebusites** = Discouragement

How to Assassinate the Assassin of Familiar Spirits

1. **Recognition of the Spirit**, Psalm 32:5; Psalm 139:23-24; Ezekiel 20:43
2. **Repentance to the Lord**, Matthew 3:2
3. **Renunciation of the Spirit**, Matthew 3:7-8; Acts 19:18-19
4. **Return to the Lord**, Zechariah 1:3

Bind: Familiar Spirits
Loose: Divine Connections
Read: Psalm 133

SPIRIT OF JEALOUSY
Numbers 5:14(ESV)

"and if the spirit of jealousy comes over him and he is jealous of his wife who has defiled herself, or if the spirit of jealousy comes over him and he is jealous of his wife, though she has not defiled herself,"

Jealousy means to resent the success of others or to resent what others have. Cain first experienced jealousy of his brother Abel in Genesis 4:1-7. In Romans 13:12-14(NIV), jealousy is listed with orgies, drunkenness, and sexual immorality.

The Spirit of Jealousy is a "dividing" spirit that attempts to destroy unity in homes, churches, and friendships. It is a "driving" spirit that causes you to want to be better than others or have more of something than someone else. It will make you question why others are successful or blessed, and it'll make you wonder why you are not as successful or as blessed as them.

Three Stages of Jealousy:
1. **Begins with Resentment**
2. **Leads to Wishing for Removal**
3. **Ends with Seeking Revenge**

Ralph was driving home one evening when he suddenly realized that it was his daughter's birthday. He ran into

the toy store and said to the shop assistant, "How much is that Barbie in the window?"
In a condescending manner, she said, "Which Barbie? Gym Barbie for $19.95, Beach Barbie for $21.95, Nightclubbing Barbie for $25.95, or Divorce Barbie for $265.00."
Ralph asked, "Why is Divorced Barbie so much more expensive?"
"That obvious," the sales lady said, "Divorced Barbie comes with Ken's house, Ken's car, Ken's boat, and Ken's furniture!"

Three Examples of Jealousy:
- Cain with Abel, Genesis 4
- Joseph's 10 brothers sold him into slavery because their father loved Joseph more, Genesis 37
- Saul was jealous towards David after he killed Goliath and the people gave more praise to David than to Saul

The cause of jealousy is found in Genesis 4:3-7. Jealousy is caused when people are intimated by someone's strengths and made conscious of their own shortcomings.

> *"And in process of time it came to pass, that Cain brought of the fruit of the ground an offering unto the Lord.*
> *And Abel, he also brought of the firstlings of his flock and of the fat thereof. And*

the Lord had respect unto Abel and to his offering:
But unto Cain and to his offering he had not respect. And Cain was very wroth, and his countenance fell.
And the Lord said unto Cain, Why art thou wroth? and why is thy countenance fallen?
If thou doest well, shalt thou not be accepted? and if thou doest not well, sin lieth at the door. And unto thee shall be his desire, and thou shalt rule over him."
Genesis 4:3-7

> **The consequence of jealousy not being dealt with will always result in loss and unfulfillment in your life.**

The Bible doesn't tell us why Cain's offering was rejected other than His offering came from the ground, which was cursed by God because of Adam and Eve's sin. His attitude was not one of love but of duty. Proverbs 21:27 says, *"The sacrifice of the wicked is an abomination to God."* He was going through the motions. He brought his first fruit and was doing it as an obligation. Even in verse 7, God gave Cain a second chance to bring an acceptable offering, but he refused.

Characteristics of Jealousy

- Vengeful, Proverbs 6:34
- Insecure, Deuteronomy 31:16
- Competitive, Genesis 4:4-5
- Envious, Proverbs 14:30
- Contentious, Proverbs 13:10
- Hatred, 1 Thessalonians 4:8
- Murder, Genesis 4:8
- Anger, Genesis 4:5-6
- Suspicious, Genesis 37:8
- Distrustful, Acts 15:37-38
- Selfish, Philippians 2:3
- Materialistic, Proverbs 15:27
- Thieves, 1 Corinthians 6:10
- Cannot handle correction, 1Thessalonians 4:8

Jealousy will cause us to:

1. **Compare Ourselves to Others**
   2 Corinthians 10:12; Compare is to examine in order to note similarities and differences.

2. **Compete with Others**
   Compete is to strive with another to achieve a goal. Stop trying to keep up with other people. Jealous people never want to lose a game, things, looks (which can lead to eating disorders), and arguments.

3. **Criticize Others**
Galatians 5:14-15; Criticizing others is finding fault with others. Even constructive criticism could be destructive jealousy, if not done in a proper God-motivated manner. Miriam criticized Moses and ended up with leprosy.

Consequences of Jealousy
Genesis 4:10-16

"And he said, What hast thou done? the voice of thy brother's blood crieth unto me from the ground.
And now art thou cursed from the earth, which hath opened her mouth to receive thy brother's blood from thy hand;
When thou tillest the ground, it shall not henceforth yield unto thee her strength; a fugitive and a vagabond shalt thou be in the earth.
And Cain said unto the Lord, My punishment is greater than I can bear.
Behold, thou hast driven me out this day from the face of the earth; and from thy face shall I be hid; and I shall be a fugitive and a vagabond in the earth; and it shall come to pass, that every one that findeth me shall slay me.
And the Lord said unto him, Therefore whosoever slayeth Cain, vengeance shall be taken on him sevenfold. And the Lord set a

mark upon Cain, lest any finding him should kill him.
And Cain went out from the presence of the Lord, and dwelt in the land of Nod, on the east of Eden."

The consequences of jealousy not being dealt with will always result in loss and unfulfillment in your life.

How to Assassinate the Assassin of Jealousy

1. **Learn to be Content,** Philippians 4:11.
2. **Rejoice with Those Who Get Blessed,** Luke 1:42-43.
3. **Learn to Overcome Evil with Good,** Romans 12:19-21.
4. **Live to Love, and Love to Give.** Jealousy has no place in a loving and giving heart.
5. **If Possible, Go to the Person You Have Been Jealous of and Confess and Ask for Forgiveness,** James 5:16.

Bind: A Spirit of Jealousy
Loose: Contentment
Read: Philippians 4:11-13

SPIRIT OF HEAVINESS
Isaiah 61:3

"To appoint unto them that mourn in Zion, to give unto them beauty for ashes, the oil of joy for mourning, the garment of praise for the spirit of heaviness; that they might be called trees of righteousness, the planting of the Lord, that he might be glorified."

Heaviness is an abnormal state of perpetual grief and discouragement. The National Institute of Mental Health says, "One in five people suffer from depression." The Spirit of Heaviness is one of the easiest spirits to detect, but it is one of the hardest to get delivered from.

> *"A merry heart maketh a cheerful countenance; but by sorrow of the heart the spirit is broken."* Proverbs 15:13

Two Kinds of Heaviness

1. **Grief Because of a Loss.**
2. **Discouragement Because Things Are Not Going the Way We Planned or Like.**

It is normal to have a period of mourning after the loss of a loved one, a favorite possession, pet, job position, boyfriend, or girlfriend. When we lose something we value, it takes time to adjust. Grief is a way to empty out the deep feelings that must not be kept inside.

Three Essentials for Recovering From a Great Loss
- Tears
- Talk
- Time

"Surely he hath bourne our griefs, and carried our sorrows: yet we did esteem him stricken, smitten of God, and afflicted." Isaiah 53:4,

"Brethren, I count not myself to have apprehended: but this one thing I do, forgetting those things which are behind, and reaching forth unto those things which are before, I press toward the mark for the prize of the high calling of God in Christ Jesus." Philippians 3:13-14

Characteristics of a Spirit of Heaviness

The mission of this spirit is to rob you of your joy and then to produce evil fruit through these manifestations.

- Excessive mourning and grief
- Impatience
- Rejection

- Self-pity, Psalm 69:20
- Depression
- Hopelessness
- Worry
- Loneliness; they isolate instead of insulate
- Anger
- Insomnia, Nehemiah 2:2
- Paranoid
- Suicidal thoughts
- Gluttony

> *Put on the garment of praise, and apply the oil of joy.*

Isaiah assures us that God will turn our "ashes", or death experiences, into something of beauty. He does it when we put on the garment of praise, and apply the oil of joy to our aching heart. The greatest anti-depressant in the world is praising God.

How to Assassinate the Assassin of Heaviness

1. **Return to the Lord,** Joel 2:13
   "Therefore say thou unto them, Thus saith the Lord of hosts; Turn ye unto me, saith the Lord of hosts, and I will turn unto you, saith

the Lord of hosts." Zechariah 1:3

2. Repent

"Repent ye therefore, and be converted, that your sins may be blotted out, when the times of refreshing shall come from the presence of the Lord." Acts 3:19

3. Remember Your Good Past

"Then beware lest thou forget the Lord, which brought thee forth out of the land of Egypt, from the house of bondage." Deuteronomy 6:12

4. Release Your Praise, Psalm 43:5

"When I remember these things, I pour out my soul in me: for I had gone with the multitude, I went with them to the house of God, with the voice of joy and praise, with a multitude that kept holyday. Why art thou cast down, O my soul? and why art thou disquieted in me? hope thou in God: for I shall yet praise him for the help of his countenance." Psalm 42:4-5

Bind: Spirit of Heaviness
Loose: Comforter, Garment Of Praise, and Oil Of Joy.
Read: John 15:26; Isaiah 61:3

SPIRIT OF WHOREDOM
Hosea 4:12

"My people ask counsel at their stocks, and their staff declareth unto them: for the spirit of whoredoms hath caused them to err, and they have gone a whoring from under their God."

Whoredom means to sell oneself for unworthy, ungodly, and unprofitable purposes. Three of Hosea's children's names represent the outcome that falls upon spiritual harlots:

1. Jezreel - means judgment; your flesh rules your spirit instead of your spirit ruling your flesh.
2. Lo-Ruhmah - means without grace; you won't have grace.
3. Lo-Ammi - means not my people or illegitimate; you'll be illegitimate

Two of the three probably were not Hosea's children.

A 2006 magazine article listed some trends the church was moving toward showing how a spirit of whoredom has impacted our churches:

- Moving away from an emphasis on children and youth.
- Moving away from preaching on purity, holiness, and the blood of Jesus.

As long as I'm around, we are not going to compromise and be a politically correct, seeker-friendly church that follows the trends of the world.

Characteristics of a Spirit of Whoredom

- Unfaithfulness
- Unbelief- relying on human resources rather than Heavenly resources
- Lack of discipline
- Fear of commitment
- Love of money, Psalm 15:27
- Chronic dissatisfaction
- Love of position
- Spiritual adultery
- Excessive appetite, 1 Corinthians 6:13-20
- Love of body

How to Assassinate the Assassin of a Spirit of Whoredom

When it comes to returning to a right relationship with the Lord, Psalm 37:27 sums it up. *"Depart from evil, and do good; and dwell for evermore."*

1. **Depart from Evil**
2. **Do Good**
3. **Dwell Forevermore**

Sometimes the most powerful answers are just the simplest ones.

Bind: Unfaithfulness
Loose: A Desire to be Faithful
Read: Psalm 86:11

RELIGIOUS SPIRIT
2 Timothy 3:5

"Having a form of godliness, but denying the power thereof: from such turn away."

The Pharisees were kept out of the presence of the Lord, and the promises of God were held back from them; not because of God, but because of their own doing. In order to walk in the presence of God and receive His promises, you must do two things:

1. **Have an Experience with Christ**
2. **Apply the Expertise of Christ**

It's not enough to know the person; you have to apply the principles. A Religious Spirit is an evil spirit that substitutes religious activity for the true power of the Holy Spirit. The number one spirit Jesus had to deal with in His ministry was a Religious Spirit. A Religious Spirit is listed among 19 things we are commanded to beware of in the last days. Most of the time a Religious Spirit is founded on a zeal

> *The #1 spirit Jesus had to deal with in His ministry was a Religious Spirit.*

for God. No one on earth had a greater zeal than the Pharisees, but they opposed everything Jesus did in Romans 10:2.

Characteristics of a Religious Spirit

- A sense that you are closer to God than other people
- A tendency to see your primary mission is to tear down what you feel is wrong
- Unable to receive correction (unteachable)
- Overwhelming guilt that you can never measure up to the Lord's standards
- Doing things so people will notice
- A rejection of things you don't understand
    - Tongues
    - Gifts
    - Going down in the Spirit
- Embarrassed or repulsed by demonstrations of spiritual emotionalism like David's wife, Michal. Just because something is emotional, doesn't make it spiritual, but when it's spiritual, it will affect your emotions
- Suspicious of new people in the church
- Unwilling to accept new ideas or approaches

How to Assassinate the Assassin of a Religious Spirit

1. **Hate Religion of Man**
2. **Love a Relationship with God**
3. **Humble Yourself and Realize You Don't Have to Have All the Answers**
4. **Don't Reject What You Don't Understand**
5. **Embrace New Ideas and New People**
6. **Pray for True Manifestations of the Holy Spirit**
7. **Be Real; Never Fake**

Bind: Ritualistic Religious Practices
Loose: True Relationship with Christ
Read: 2 Timothy 3:5

SPIRIT OF ABSALOM
2 Samuel 15

"And Absalom said unto him, See, thy matters are good and right; but there is no man deputed of the king to hear thee. Absalom said moreover, Oh that I were made judge in the land, that every man which hath any suit or cause might come unto me, and I would do him justice! And it was so, that when any man came nigh to him to do him obeisance, he put forth his hand, and took him, and kissed him. And on this manner did Absalom to all Israel that came to the king for judgment: so Absalom stole the hearts of the men of Israel." 2 Samuel 15:3-6

Absalom was the 3rd son of King David, and he is described in 2 Samuel 14:25 as *"the most handsome man in the kingdom"*. The Bible also mentions his long-flowing hair as one of his most striking features. Absalom was confident, full of charisma, and a tremendous natural leader. He also had a desire for revenge that surfaced when he had his brother killed for raping his sister. A streak of rebellion ran through the core of his being, as he was unwilling to do the necessary things to legitimately inherit his father's kingdom. After having his brother killed, he was the oldest son and became next in line to the throne, but because of his envy for David's power and position, Absalom led a revolt against his own father that temporarily drove David from the throne.

Although Absalom is dead, the spirit that ruled him is still around and attempts to attach itself to others in order to dethrone and discredit the legitimate things of God. We need to be aware of the Absalom spirit. So, I've made a partial list of characteristics to help you identify this spirit when it surfaces.

Characteristics of an Absalom Spirit

- It surfaces in divisiveness and negative criticism of authority, 2 Samuel 5:3
- It revolves around selfish ambition that can be disguised in service to others, 2 Samuel 15:2
- Its goal is to "dethrone" the legitimate and replace the one in authority, 2 Samuel 15
- It creates distrust in god-appointed authority, 2 Samuel 13:20-21
- It uses looks, gifts, personality, guilt, and all types of manipulation to gain an advantage, 2 Samuel 14-15
- It is rooted in bitterness because of unresolved issues, anger, disappointment, fear, or offenses, 2 Samuel 13:22

- It disguises itself in hidden agendas and secret alliances, 2 Samuel 13:22-29
- It manifests in betrayal and disloyalty, 2 Samuel 15:12

The Absalom spirit is often birthed in incompetent, rebellious, people who have an unwillingness to be held accountable. It secretly brings division by creating distrust and revealing flaws about the authority of the house. Ultimately, Absalom didn't prevail in his conspiracy against his father. Although David was driven out, he regrouped by gathering his troops and ran Absalom out on a fast-moving mule. His long-flowing hair got caught in an oak tree, and he hung from the tree by his hair until he was fatally pierced with three darts by Joab, one of David's captains. His body was taken down and buried in a pit in the middle of a forest. The Bible said in 2 Samuel 18:18 that Absalom was childless. He was barren physically, spiritually, and historically with the only monument to his legacy of rebellion being a premature death and a pile of stones raised over his grave.

Resist rebellion, offense, and the desire to undermine authority. Beware of this spirit. It will come and attempt to rear its ugly head in your church, business, home, and relationships.

How to Assassinate the Assassin of an Absalom Spirit

1. Deal with Offense Quickly
2. Do not Participate in Secret Meetings
3. Pray for Your Leaders
4. Stay Humble
5. Be Accountable to Authority
6. Embrace Correction
7. Don't be Critical; be Supportive
8. Expose Evil

Keep your heart connected to the heart of God, and know you can't curse what God has blessed.

Bind: Division
Loose: Unity
Read: 1 Corinthians 1:6

SPIRIT OF SAUL
1 Samuel 18

"And Saul was very wroth, and the saying displeased him; and he said, They have ascribed unto David ten thousands, and to me they have ascribed but thousands: and what can he have more but the kingdom? And Saul eyed David from that day and forward." 1 Samuel 18:8-9

We see the Spirit of Saul in full character here in 1 Samuel 18. The main theme of this chapter is the spirit that controlled Saul and drove his flesh to want to destroy David, who was a man after God's own heart. Saul was controlling and extremely jealous of other people's success. He took credit for victories he wasn't even involved in. He also tried to shut up and kill the prophetic voice of God. Be aware of others who are uncomfortable around the anointed of God.

Characteristics of a Spirit of Saul

- Attempts to control others, verse 2
- Is intimidated by others success, verse 5
- Is always suspicious and jealous, verse 9
- Is full of evil, verse 10
- Tries to shut up and kill the prophetic voice,

verses 11-15
- Uncomfortable around the anointing, verses 13-16
- Backs out of keeping promises, verses 17-19
- Tries to sabotage the success of others, verse 21
- Loves secrets, verse 22
- Angry and fearful, verses 8, 12, 15, and 29
- Makes unreasonable demands, verses 25-27

In 1 Samuel 12, Samuel instructed Saul on the behavior of a King. Samuel had a foolproof plan for Saul to go to another level in his walk with the Lord and in his rule as king. Throughout chapter 13, Saul rejected the teaching of the man of God and through disobedience proved he was not a man after God's own heart. Although he ruled as King until his death, he lost his kingdom that day because he was unwilling to accept and apply godly principles to his life. He cursed himself and left behind a mess for his family because of his true character. Saul hated David because David was willing to do what Saul himself was not willing to do. David followed the foolproof plan of Samuel which proved he was a man after God's own heart. If you can relate to the characteristics of Saul, then it's time to bind those characteristics and loose the characteristics of David, a man after God's own heart.

How to Assassinate the Assassin of a Spirit of Saul

1. Praises Others and Put them Above Yourself
2. Be a Person of Faith
3. Be a Person of Obedience
4. Be a Person of Loyalty
5. Be a Person of Patience
6. Want God Things Not "Good" Things
7. Influence Others Toward Righteousness
8. Admits When You are Wrong
9. Be Teachable and Receive Correction
10. Teach Others Wisdom so They Will Lean on the Lord and Not You

Bind: A Spirit of Saul
Loose: A Spirit of David
Read: 1 Samuel 13:1-22

CHAPTER

GOOD SPIRITS OF THE BIBLE
---

1. **Spirit of Wisdom and Understanding**

   "And the spirit of the LORD shall rest upon him, the spirit of wisdom and understanding, the spirit of counsel and might, the spirit of knowledge and of the fear of the LORD;" Isaiah 11:2

2. **Spirit of Counsel and Might**

   "And the spirit of the LORD shall rest upon him, the spirit of wisdom and understanding, the spirit of counsel and might, the spirit of knowledge and of the fear of the LORD;" Isaiah 11:2

3. **Spirit of Knowledge and of the Fear of the Lord**

   "And the spirit of the Lord shall rest upon him, the spirit of wisdom and understanding, the spirit of counsel and might, the spirit of

knowledge and of the fear of the Lord;" Isaiah 11:2

4. Spirit of Wisdom and Revelation

"That the God of our Lord Jesus Christ, the Father of glory, may give unto you the spirit of wisdom and revelation in the knowledge of him" Ephesians 1:17

5. Spirit of Truth

"We are of God: he that knoweth God heareth us; he that is not of God heareth not us. Hereby know we the spirit of truth, and the spirit of error." 1 John 4:6

6. Faithful Spirit

"A talebearer revealeth secrets: but he that is of a faithful spirit concealeth the matter." Proverbs 11:13

7. Humble Spirit

"Better it is to be of an humble spirit with the lowly, than to divide the spoil with the proud." Proverbs 16:19

8. Excellent Spirit

"He that hath knowledge spareth his words: and a man of understanding is of an excellent spirit." Proverbs 17:27

9. Spirit of Grace and Supplication

"And I will pour upon the house of David, and upon the inhabitants of Jerusalem, the spirit of grace and of supplications: and they shall look upon me whom they have pierced, and they shall mourn for him, as one mourneth for his only son, and shall be in bitterness for him, as one that is in bitterness for his firstborn." Zechariah 12:10

10. Spirit of Adoption

"For ye have not received the spirit of bondage again to fear; but ye have received the Spirit of adoption, whereby we cry, Abba, Father." Romans 8:15

11. Spirit of Promise

"In whom ye also trusted, after that ye heard the word of truth, the gospel of your salvation: in whom also after that ye believed, ye were sealed with that holy Spirit of promise," Ephesians 1:13

12. The Holy Spirit

"But the Comforter, which is the Holy Ghost, whom the Father will send in my

name, he shall teach you all things, and bring all things to your remembrance, whatsoever I have said unto you." John 14:26

13. Spirit of Power, Love and a Sound Mind

"For God hath not given us the spirit of fear; but of power, and of love, and of a sound mind." 2 Timothy 1:7

14. Contrite Spirit

"For thus saith the high and lofty One that inhabiteth eternity, whose name is Holy; I dwell in the high and holy place, with him also that is of a contrite and humble spirit, to revive the spirit of the humble, and to revive the heart of the contrite ones." Isaiah 57:15

15. Good Spirit

"Teach me to do thy will; for thou art my God: thy spirit is good; lead me into the land of uprightness." Psalm 143:10

16. Meek and Quiet Spirit

"But let it be the hidden man of the heart, in that which is not corruptible, even the ornament of a meek and quiet spirit, which is in the sight of God of great price." 1 Peter 3:4

17. Spirit of Prophecy

"And I fell at his feet to worship him. And he said unto me, See thou do it not: I am thy fellowservant, and of thy brethren that have the testimony of Jesus: worship God: for the testimony of Jesus is the spirit of prophecy." Revelation 19:10

18. Patient Spirit

"Better is the end of a thing than the beginning thereof: and the patient in spirit is better than the proud in spirit." Ecclesiastes 7:8

19. Stirred Spirit

"Now while Paul waited for them at Athens, his spirit was stirred in him, when he saw the city wholly given to idolatry." Acts 17:16

20. Fervent Spirit

"Not slothful in business; fervent in spirit; serving the Lord;" Romans 12:11

21. Purposed Spirit

"After these things were ended, Paul purposed in the spirit, when he had passed through Macedonia and Achaia, to go to Jerusalem, saying, After I have been there, I must also see Rome." Acts 19:21

22. Quickening Spirit

"And so it is written, The first man Adam was made a living soul; the last Adam was made a quickening spirit."
1 Corinthians 15:45

23. Spirit of Unity

"Endeavouring to keep the unity of the Spirit in the bond of peace." Ephesians 4:3

24. Free Spirit

"Restore unto me the joy of thy salvation; and uphold me with thy free spirit." Psalm 51:12

25. New Spirit

"And I will give them one heart, and I will put a new spirit within you; and I will take the stony heart out of their flesh, and will give them an heart of flesh:" Ezekiel 11:19

26. Refreshed Spirit

"For they have refreshed my spirit and yours: therefore acknowledge ye them that are such." 1 Corinthians 16:18

27. Spirit of Faith

"We having the same spirit of faith, according as it is written, I believed, and therefore have I spoken; we also believe, and therefore speak;" 2 Corinthians 4:13

28. Spirit of Glory

"If ye be reproached for the name of Christ, happy are ye; for the spirit of glory and of God resteth upon you: on their part he is evil spoken of, but on your part he is glorified." 1 Peter 4:14

29. Spirit of Life

"For the law of the Spirit of life in Christ Jesus hath made me free from the law of sin and death." Romans 8:2

30. Spirit of Meekness

"Brethren, if a man be overtaken in a fault, ye which are spiritual, restore such an one in the spirit of meekness; considering thyself, lest thou also be tempted." Galatians 6:1

Pray for these good spirits to be an active part of your everyday life. You should never be at a loss of what to pray for in your life, but this list will certainly help you to stay on the right track. Believe for these good spirits to help you achieve great success.

CHAPTER 7

KEEPING YOUR FREEDOM

Jesus was very clear that living a separated life unto the Lord would never exempt us from trouble in the world. We also need to remember that once we turn our lives over to Christ, the enemy will do whatever he can to get us back serving him. Life is war!! We must wage this Holy War with the spiritual weapons we have been given to defeat the enemy. Here is a comprehensive list of how to fight and win the war against spiritual assassins.

How to Keep Your Deliverance

1. **Put on the Whole Armor of God,** Ephesians 6:10-18
    - Belt of Truth
    - Breastplate of Righteousness
    - Shoes of Peace
    - Shield of Faith
    - Helmet of Salvation
    - The Sword of the Spirit or Word of God
    - Pray in Tongues

2. **Make Positive Confessions,** Mark 11:23; Romans 2:4
   Negative words are open doors for the enemy to enter and influence your life.

3. **Have a Vision,** Proverbs 29:18
   Look forward to what God has promised, and never look back.

4. **Use Prayer Cloths,** Acts 19:11-12
   Paul used prayer cloths as a point of contact with the anointing. Prayer cloths are great ways to secretly influence others who are demonically bound. Put them in other people's cars, clothes pockets, pillow cases, and jeans.

5. **Meditate on the Scriptures,** Psalm 1:1-3

6. **Deny Your Flesh,** Luke 9:23

7. **Get Filled with the Holy Spirit,** Acts 2

8. **Be Accountable to Authority,** Hebrews 10:25

9. **Use the Keys to the Kingdom,** Matthew 16:18-19
   - Binding
   - Loosing
   - Name of Jesus
   - Blood of Jesus
   - Your Personal Testimony

10. Love Others, 1 Peter 3:1; 1 Corinthians 13
Love is our greatest weapon!!

11. Develop a Lifestyle of Practicing Prayer and Praise, 1 Thessalonians 5:17

12. Set and Enforce Boundaries, Numbers 34:1-2; Joshua 13:1-33

13. Prophetic Prayer, Romans 4:17
Call things that are not as you want them to be according to God's Word and Will.

14. Fellowship with Like-Minded Believers, 2 Corinthians 6:14

15. Fasting, Matthew 17:21

If you make application of these 15 practices into your life, there is no doubt you will remain free. Freedom is given by God, but it's up to us, as individuals, to maintain our freedom.

> *"So shall they fear the name of the Lord from the west, and his glory from the rising of the sun. When the enemy shall come in like a flood, the Spirit of the Lord shall lift up a standard against him."* Isaiah 59:19

CHAPTER

SPIRITUAL WARFARE AMMUNITION

Here are some of the best scriptures in the Bible to use as ammunition to fire back at the enemy when you are under attack:

> *"But the Lord is faithful, who shall stablish you, and keep you from evil."*
> 2 Thessalonians 3:3

> *"Ye are of God, little children, and have overcome them: because greater is he that is in you, than he that is in the world."*
> 1 John 4:4

> *"The LORD shall cause thine enemies that rise up against thee to be smitten before thy face: they shall come out against thee one way, and flee before thee seven ways."* Deuteronomy 28:7

> *"And they overcame him by the blood of the Lamb, and by the word of their*

testimony; and they loved not their lives unto the death." Revelation 12:11

"And I say also unto thee, That thou art Peter, and upon this rock I will build my church; and the gates of hell shall not prevail against it." Matthew 16:18

"One man of you shall chase a thousand: for the L{\scriptsize ORD} *your God, he it is that fighteth for you, as he hath promised you."* Joshua 23:10

"What shall we then say to these things? If God be for us, who can be against us?" Romans 8:31

"Have not I commanded thee? Be strong and of a good courage; be not afraid, neither be thou dismayed: for the L{\scriptsize ORD} *thy God is with thee whithersoever thou goest."* Joshua 1:9

"He that dwelleth in the secret place of the most High shall abide under the shadow of the Almighty. I will say of the L{\scriptsize ORD}, *He is my refuge and my fortress: my God; in him will I trust. Surely he shall deliver thee from the snare of the fowler, and from the noisome pestilence. He shall cover thee with his*

feathers, and under his wings shalt thou trust: his truth shall be thy shield and buckler." Psalm 91:1-4

"Ye shall not need to fight in this battle: set yourselves, stand ye still, and see the salvation of the LORD with you, O Judah and Jerusalem: fear not, nor be dismayed; to morrow go out against them: for the LORD will be with you."
2 Chronicles 20:17

"And ye shall know the truth, and the truth shall make you free." John 8:32

"But they that wait upon the LORD shall renew their strength; they shall mount up with wings as eagles; they shall run, and not be weary; and they shall walk, and not faint." Isaiah 40:31

"And having spoiled principalities and powers, he made a shew of them openly, triumphing over them in it."
Colossians 2:15

"He that committeth sin is of the devil; for the devil sinneth from the beginning. For this purpose the Son of God was manifested, that he might destroy the works of the devil." 1 John 3:8

"Submit yourselves therefore to God. Resist the devil, and he will flee from you." James 4:7

"For though we walk in the flesh, we do not war after the flesh: (For the weapons of our warfare are not carnal, but mighty through God to the pulling down of strong holds;) Casting down imaginations, and every high thing that exalteth itself against the knowledge of God, and bringing into captivity every thought to the obedience of Christ;"
2 Corinthians 10:3-5

"Be sober, be vigilant; because your adversary the devil, as a roaring lion, walketh about, seeking whom he may devour: Whom resist stedfast in the faith, knowing that the same afflictions are accomplished in your brethren that are in the world." 1 Peter 5:8-9

"No weapon that is formed against thee shall prosper; and every tongue that shall rise against thee in judgment thou shalt condemn. This is the heritage of the servants of the Lord, and their righteousness is of me, saith the Lord."
Isaiah 54:17

"Nay, in all these things we are more than conquerors through him that loved us." Romans 8:37

"But thanks be to God, which giveth us the victory through our Lord Jesus Christ." 1 Corinthians 15:57

"Then he answered and spake unto me, saying, This is the word of the Lord unto Zerubbabel, saying, Not by might, nor by power, but by my spirit, saith the Lord of hosts." Zechariah 4:6

"Behold, I give unto you power to tread on serpents and scorpions, and over all the power of the enemy: and nothing shall by any means hurt you." Luke 10:19

"The thief cometh not, but for to steal, and to kill, and to destroy: I am come that they might have life, and that they might have it more abundantly." John 10:10

"Verily I say unto you, Whatsoever ye shall bind on earth shall be bound in heaven: and whatsoever ye shall loose on earth shall be loosed in heaven. Again I say unto you, That if two of you shall agree on earth as touching any thing that they shall ask, it shall be done for them of

my Father which is in heaven."
Matthew 18:18-19

"Put on the whole armour of God, that ye may be able to stand against the wiles of the devil.

For we wrestle not against flesh and blood, but against principalities, against powers, against the rulers of the darkness of this world, against spiritual wickedness in high places.

Wherefore take unto you the whole armour of God, that ye may be able to withstand in the evil day, and having done all, to stand.

Stand therefore, having your loins girt about with truth, and having on the breastplate of righteousness;

And your feet shod with the preparation of the gospel of peace;

Above all, taking the shield of faith, wherewith ye shall be able to quench all the fiery darts of the wicked.

And take the helmet of salvation, and the sword of the Spirit, which is the word of God:

Praying always with all prayer and supplication in the Spirit, and watching thereunto with all perseverance and supplication for all saints;"
Ephesians 6:11-18

CONCLUSION

There is no doubt that spiritual assassins are assigned to all of us in order to destroy us. We must not be devil-conscious but remain God-conscious in pursuit of our relationship with Christ. We have to stay connected to the Holy Spirit to discern the problem and use the symptoms described in this book to determine our need for deliverance. I have made every effort to define and describe all the spiritual assassins of the Bible. I have included Biblical tools for you to use to win the battle. We can't accommodate the devil; we must confront him with every Godly weapon we have been given. As we identify the specific spirit that is attempting to get the best of us, it's then we can apply the truths to our lives, so we can be victorious.

We are not just living in the last of the last days, but we are living in the final hours before the return of Christ. With this in mind, we must not be caught off guard by the enemy's attacks. They will become even more fierce as he realizes time is short. We must close the gap and minimize the distance between us and the Lord on a daily basis. The closer we come to knowing the Lord, the more we understand what we need to stop doing in order to be successful.

My prayer for you is to have divine success from the Lord. In order to achieve this, you must cooperate with the Lord and do your part. The battle is great; the enemy is fighting, but always remember, greater is He that is within you than he that is in the world.

> *"I have fought a good fight, I have finished my course, I have kept the faith:"*
> *2 Timothy 4:7*

www.ingramcontent.com/pod-product-compliance
Lightning Source LLC
Chambersburg PA
CBHW072335300426
44109CB00042B/1624